The Great Big Golden
Make It & Do It
Book

 **Golden Press • New York**

Western Publishing Company, Inc.
Racine, Wisconsin

Copyright © Marshall Cavendish Ltd., 1978
All rights reserved.
This book may not be sold outside
the United States of America, its territories and Canada.
First U.S.A. edition, 1980
No part of this book may be reproduced or copied in any form
without written permission from the publisher.
Printed in the U.S.A. by Western Publishing Company, Inc.
GOLDEN®, A GOLDEN BOOK® and GOLDEN PRESS® are trademarks of
Western Publishing Company, Inc.
Library of Congress Catalog Card Number: 79-89504

Useful things to know

There are 365 projects in this book and many different materials are used. Here are a few: tin cans, matchboxes, bottles and jars, lollipop or ice cream sticks, paper bags, nuts and bolts, corks, pebbles, shells, thread spools and buttons. Some other important ones are explained on these two pages. So don't throw anything away! Save old newspapers and magazines, too. Use spare ones to cover your work surface.

All the things you will need for a particular project appear in **bold letters like these.** Read through each project first, then get together all the things you will need. And remember to clean up after you have finished!

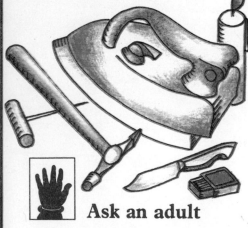

Ask an adult

When you see the sign of a hand in the border of a project, *always* ask an adult to help. The hand is a warning *never* to use the tools or materials listed here on your own:

Nails for punching holes and for building.
A hammer for banging nails.
An awl for punching holes.

An iron for pressing leaves or fabric.
Long matches for science experiments.
Candles, lighted with a match.
A penknife for cutting thick materials.
Glass for building projects.
Matches, if they need to be struck.
You will also see **"ask an adult"** to remind you not to take things which don't belong to you without asking permission first.

Drawing tools

You will find these materials in a stationery or art supply store.
Felt-tipped pens can be used on paper or cardboard instead of paints.
Wax crayons can also be used to color paper and cardboard and can cover over other colors.
Waterproof India ink *must be used with great care* as it won't wash off if you spill it on anything.
A compass is very useful whenever you need to draw a circle of a particular size.

Paper and cardboard

Paper and cardboard can be bought at a stationery or art supply store.
Tracing paper is see-through.
Wax paper won't let sticky things cling to it. (It can also be used for tracing.)
Gummed paper shapes have paper backs which you peel off to get a sticky surface.
Cardboard comes in all colors and thicknesses. The project will tell you if you need a special kind (stiff or thin, for instance).
Sandpaper has a rough surface and is used for smoothing off cut edges of wood. Buy it from a hardware store.

Paint and varnish

Wherever you see **paint** in a project you will also need a **paintbrush** (unless the project states otherwise).
Acrylic paint can be used on paper and cardboard, and on top of other paints and hard surfaces, such as wood. Wash brushes in water before the paint dries.
Poster paint is easy to use and brushes can be washed in water. Buy these in an art supply or toy store.
Paint means house paint. Wash brushes in **turpentine** if you use enamel house paint, but in water if you use latex paint.
Varnish is used to give surfaces a long lasting, shiny finish. Polyurethane varnish is best. Wash brushes in turpentine.
You can buy these in a hardware store.

Fasteners

Map pins are short pins with small, round, colored heads.
Thumbtacks are stronger and have big heads.
Paper clips hold lightweight paper or cardboard together.
Paper fasteners have two prongs which you push through paper or cardboard, then bend outward.
Pins are ordinary straight ones.
Safety pins are ones with a catch. Buy these in a dime store.
Staples are three-sided metal fasteners used for holding wire mesh to a frame.
Corrugated fasteners are pieces of ridged metal which hold joints of wood together.
Buy these last two kinds at a hardware store.

Glues and tapes

Buy these at a stationery or hardware store.

Glue means any ordinary glue, such as paper paste, that will stick paper and thin cardboard.

Household cement is used for sticking heavier materials together.

Wood glue sticks wood together.

White glue is used for sticking cloth, beads, braid or yarn to other surfaces.

Masking tape is used to stick things to walls or windows without leaving marks. Don't fix it too firmly and avoid paper surfaces.

Sewing things

These may be bought in the notions department of a department store or in a sewing supply store.

Knitting needles are the ones used for making sweaters.

Darning needles have big eyes to take yarn and are sharp.

Tapestry needles also have big eyes, but are blunt.

Cheesecloth is a very fine, net-like cloth.

Embroidery thread is shiny and thicker than sewing thread.

Shirring elastic is very thin.

Dressmaker's chalk is used for marking fabric.

Wood

You can buy most kinds of wood in a lumber yard.

Plywood is made up of layers of wood glued together.

Exterior plywood has a special surface finish so that it can be left out-of-doors.

Pine is inexpensive and nails and screws go into it easily.

Half-round molding is a thin strip of wood with one rounded side.

Doweling is always round.

Bamboo and cane rods are very light. Buy them at a gardening center or plant shop.

Wire

Wire mesh is made up of strands of wire woven together like a net.

Galvanized wire is the kind that doesn't rust.
Buy these at a hardware store.

Electrical wire has a plastic cover.

Fuse wire is fine metal thread. Buy these at an electrical supply store.

Garden wire is usually green. Buy it at a garden center or plant shop.

Other things

Plaster of Paris is a powder that sets hard when mixed with water and left (the drying time will vary according to how much is used and whether the air is dry or damp). *Never pour left over plaster down the sink.*

Self-hardening clay also sets hard. Don't put it in a warm place to hurry it up or the edges will curl. You will have to work fast with this clay or it will set before you are ready.

Plasticine can be reused. Buy these in a craft or toy store.

Magnets can be bought in a hardware or toy store.

Bulb, bulb holder, battery can all be bought in an electrical supply store or hardware store.

Basic shapes

You'll find an introduction to basic, flat shapes around the edges of these pages – and hints on how to make them three-dimensional.

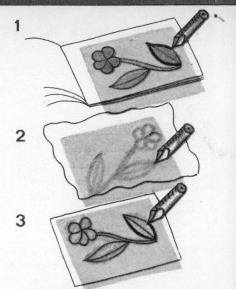

How to trace

1. Put the paper over the design or pattern on the page of the book and draw the outline of the pattern on it.

2. Turn the tracing paper over and put it on a piece of **scrap paper.** Scribble over the outline.

3. Put the tracing right side up, on a **clean sheet of paper,** and draw around the outline again.

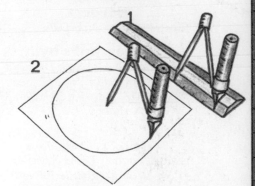

Drawing a circle

1. Set the arms of a **compass** against a **ruler** and measure the distance of the radius of the circle you want.

2. Put the pin arm on the **paper or cardboard** to mark the center of the circle.

Swing the **pencil** arm around to draw a complete circle.

Magic
Compiled by: *Peter Eldin*
Illustrated by: *Grahame Corbett*

Nature
Compiled by: *Chris Maynard*
Illustrated by: *Barbara Firth*

Crafts
Compiled by: *Eve Barwell*
Illustrated by: *Chris Legee,*
Neil Lorimer, Janet Allen, Victoria Drew

Science
Compiled by: *Neil Thomson*
Illustrated by: *Tony Hannaford*

Games
Compiled by: *Richard Kennedy*
Illustrated by: *Phil Dobson*

Hobbies
Compiled by: *Pinkie Martin*
Illustrated by: *Janet Allen*

Puzzles
Compiled by: *Bruce Leigh*
Illustrated by: *Malcolm Livingstone*

Cover
Illustration by: *Victoria Drew*

Borders
Illustration by: *Niki Daly*

Photographs by:
Steve Bicknell 274, Alun Duns 273
Peter Heinz 260, 317
Neil Lorimer 56, 57, 173, 193, 203, 295, 338, 359
Dick Miller 9, 190, 243

Editor: *Wendy Boase*
Assistant editor: *Diana Reynolds*
Art director: *Amelia Edwards*
Designer: *Jacky Paynter*
Art editor: *Sue Llewellyn*

About this book

This colorful book is packed with 365 exciting things to make and play. There's something for everybody between seven and twelve years old – for rainy indoor days, outdoor days, or just those "What-shall-I-do-next?" days.

You'll find seven different kinds of projects: magical performances, nature-watching, crafts, scientific fun, games to play, hobbies to amuse you, and puzzles to work out. You can identify each one of them by the color behind the number above each project. There's also a code guide:

easy   **harder**
    not-so-easy   **ask an adult**

Dip in wherever you like or begin at the very beginning. Or you could work your way through all the easy projects first and go on to the harder ones if you use the Project Guide in the back of the book. Before you start, read about the projects on these two pages, and look through the "Useful things to know" on the next two.

Magic

This section shows you how to do magic tricks. Some performances will need secret preparations; others can be set up right before someone's eyes. When you become a practiced magician, you could put on a big magic show.

If you want to find a magic project, look for blue in the border as shown above. It will have the number of the project in it.

Nature

In this section you will learn to observe nature and to watch how things grow and change. There are also lots of ideas for making things with finds from the natural world.

Some are all-year-around projects, and others are afternoon ones.

Find all the nature projects by looking for the bright green color behind the project number.

Crafts

Craft means doing things by hand. This section shows you how to make things from many different materials in all kinds of clever ways. You can be artistic (or messy!) but you are sure to enjoy yourself, whatever happens!

Look for the color pink with a number on it when you want to do a crafts project.

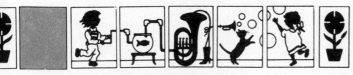

Science

Learning about science is fascinating when you make things that prove scientific laws. The science section shows you how to do this.

Some of the projects will amaze your friends; some will amuse you for hours; others can be turned into games to play.

Purple behind a number indicates that the project is a science one.

Hobbies

Saving things and searching for others is what this section is all about. Of course, you can't save things in just a day, but you can make a special display of things you have been collecting. Keep a very special hobby going forever, if you like! You will know the hobbies section by the sea-green color behind the project number.

Puzzles

Spend your quiet hours with this section. Some of the puzzles are picture ones; some are geometric; others are mathematical and a few are word puzzles. You can recognize the puzzle section by looking for the color yellow with a number on it.

The answers to most of the puzzles are in the back of the book. Don't peek first!

Games

This section really needs no explanation! Everyone plays games – sometimes on their own, sometimes with one other player, sometimes with lots of people at a party. There are all kinds to play in the games section. A few will be old favorites, others will be new and different.

When you want to play a game, look for a light-brown color above the project.

Make things move

Turn a **drinking straw** into a magic wand.
1. Dip one end of the straw in some **sugar.**
Use a **cloth** to wipe the sugar off the outside
of the straw.
2. Dip the other end of the straw in **soft soap.**
Wipe the straw again so the soap can't be seen.

★ ★ ★ ★Performance★ ★ ★ ★

Now show your friends how you can make two
matchsticks move without touching them.
3. Put **two spent matchsticks** in **water.**
4. Dip the sugared end of the straw into the
water between the matches.
The matches will move close together.
5. Dip in the soapy end of the straw.
The matches will move apart.

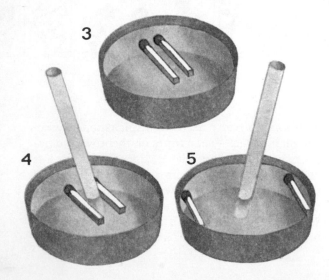

Watermark wizard

Make someone's name appear as if by magic.
1. Soak a sheet of **paper** in **water,** then put the
wet paper on a **mirror or window.**
2. Put a dry sheet of paper over the wet one.
3. With a **pencil,** write the name of your best
friend on the top sheet of paper.
4. Throw the *top sheet* away and let the
bottom sheet of paper dry.
The name on the paper will then be invisible.

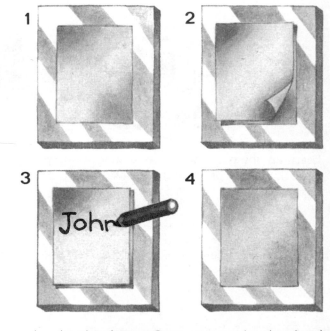

★ ★ ★ ★Performance★ ★ ★ ★

5. Hold up the sheet of paper and say that you
can make your friend's name appear on it.
6. Put the paper in a **bowl of water** and the
writing will show up.

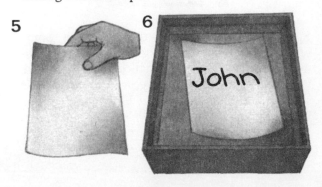

Tube of plenty

Make ribbons appear from nowhere! With **scissors,** cut a curve on a sheet of **thin cardboard** 8 inches square.
1. Paint the shape with **black poster paint.** Let the paint dry. Fold the cardboard into a cone with the black surface inside.

2. Put **cellophane tape** on the seam.
3. Cut off the tip of the cone. Cut another sheet of cardboard about 10½ inches by 6½ inches.
4. Fold the cardboard into a tube and put cellophane tape on the seam. The widest end of the cone should just fit inside the tube.

5. Use **glue** to fix the top edges of the cone and tube together.
6. When the glue is dry put some **colored ribbons** in the space between the cone and the tube.

★ ★ ★ ★ ★ ★ ★ ★ ★ ★ ★ ★ **Performance** ★ ★ ★ ★ ★ ★ ★ ★ ★ ★ ★

Hold the tube so that the ribbons face you.
7. Show everyone the other end of the tube. It will look empty. Now put the tube down on a **table.**
8. Say "Presto chango!" Then pull out the ribbons – one by one.

Inviting visitors

Making friends with small birds is quite easy if
you give them somewhere to bathe and a feeder
in your garden. Hang the feeder where cats can't
get it. Every day, leave out water and a few
fresh scraps – bread, bacon rind, cheese, apple
cores – or some bird seed. Put water in a heavy
bowl with a thick rim. Hang up half a coconut
shell, if you can get one. Clean the feeder with
a brush, sweeping out at the corners.

Bird feeder
Ask an adult to help you.
Buy a 12-inch square piece of
exterior plywood, four pieces of
quarter-round molding 10 inches by
$\frac{1}{2}$ inch, **wood glue, four nails** and
some **fine strong cord.**
1. Glue the molding to the edges
of the feeder top so that gaps are
left at each corner.
Use a **hammer** to fix a nail into
the feeder at all four corners,
leaving the heads sticking up.
2. Firmly tie a length of cord to
each nail, then wind the lengths
around the **branch of a tree.**

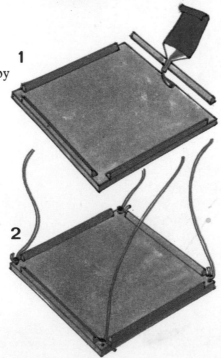

Birdbath
With a **spade,** dig a shallow hole
in a quiet, sunny part of the
garden. Use **plastic** to line the
hole, and put **stones** around the
edge to keep it in place. Or
simply sink a shallow dish into
the hole. Fill the bath with **water**
and watch how the birds play and
splash about in it.

Feathery fliers

After birds have been visiting, collect their fallen feathers, and make a mobile with them.

1. With **tracing paper** and a **pencil,** trace this little bird. Use **scissors** to cut out five birds from **colored cardboard.**

Paint eyes on each one with **poster paint** and a **brush** and stick **feathers** on with **glue.** Make a tiny hole in each bird (see dot on pattern) and tie on varying lengths of **cotton thread.**

2. Loosely tie the birds to **two bamboo or cane rods** – one 12 inches long and one 9 inches long – as shown. Tie thread to the top rod and hang up your mobile. Now slide the loose knots to and fro until the birds are perfectly balanced. Fix the knots into place by dabbing them with **nail polish.** Trim off any spare thread.

Who goes there?

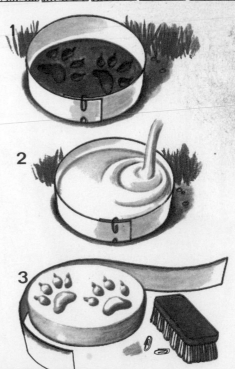

Find out which animals live in your area by taking plaster casts of their footprints. Search near rivers and ponds for tracks. Take a **bucket, wooden spoon, water, plaster of Paris, cardboard strips** 24 inches by 2½ inches, **paper clips.**

Join the ends of one cardboard strip with a paper clip.

1. Press the cardboard circle into the earth, surrounding the track. Pour water into the bucket and slowly stir in plaster until the mixture is like custard.

2. Gently pour the plaster into the circle to a depth of 1 inch. Let it dry for two hours. Carefully lift up the cardboard with the plaster cast inside.

3. At home, remove the cardboard. Clean off any mud with a **brush.** Look in an **animal book** if you don't recognize the footprint.

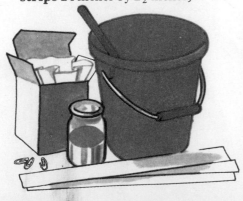

Tin can trotters

Find **two empty cans** with press-on lids
(cat food, coffee or peanut cans). Remove the
lids – you will not need them.
1. Ask an adult to punch two holes through
the bottom of each can using a **hammer** and **nail.**
2. Thread a piece of **string** 1 yard long down
through one of the holes in one can and up
through the other. Tie the ends of the string
together. Thread the second can in the same way.
Stand with one foot on each can and hold the long
loops of string in your hands. Now see how well
you can trot!

Whizzer

Turn spots into rings of color.
1. With a **pencil** draw around a **teacup** turned
upside down *once* on **stiff cardboard** and *twice*
on **white paper.** Cut out the circles with
scissors.
2. Use **glue** to stick a paper circle to each side of
the cardboard.
3. With the point of the scissors make two holes
¼ inch apart as shown.
4. Thread a piece of **string** 1½ yards long
through the holes and tie the ends.
5. Paint spots of red, yellow and blue **poster
paint** on both sides of the whizzer as shown.
Let dry.
Flick the whizzer over and over to wind it up.
Pull the string to make it whizz.

Pierrot puppet

Make a cheerful puppet on a rainy indoor day.
Cut legs and arms from **scraps of felt** with **scissors**.
Trace the pattern for the head onto **cardboard** and cut it
out. Draw a face on it with **felt-tipped pens.**
Fix the arms, legs and head to a **matchbox** with **cellophane
tape.** Stick a strip of **colored paper** all around the match-
box with **glue.**
Cut dots of felt for pompons and glue them on.
Cut three pieces of **shirring elastic** about 1 foot long.
Attach one to each hand and one to the top of the hat.
Tie the other ends to a strip of cardboard.

trace pattern

Bounce Pierrot from
the cardboard to make
him dance.

A weather vane

Meteorologists, or weather forecasters, use weather vanes to observe changes in the direction of the wind. Make one for yourself.

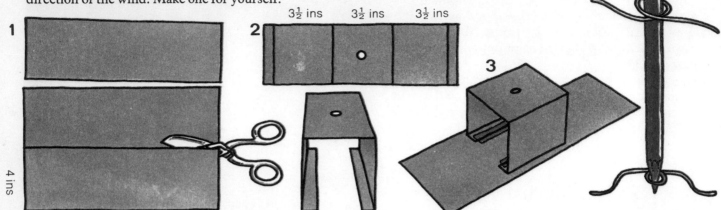

1. Use **scissors** to cut three pieces of **cardboard,** each 12 inches by 4 inches.
2. With the tip of the scissors, score across one piece of cardboard at the points shown. Make a hole in the middle with the scissors. Push a **pencil** through it until the hole is just a little bigger than the pencil. Bend the cardboard along the scored lines.

3. Use **cellophane tape** to fix the folded cardboard to one of the other pieces of cardboard. This is the stand for the weather vane. Now straighten **two paper clips.**
4. Wrap one paper clip loosely around the top of the pencil, and the other one loosely around the sharpened end. Take the paper clips off the pencil.

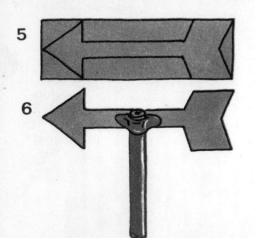

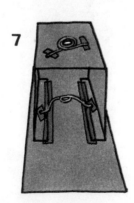

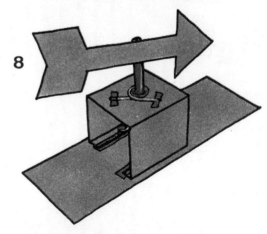

5. Draw an arrow, like the one shown, on the third piece of cardboard. Cut out the shape.
6. Use **plasticine** to fix the pencil to the center of the arrow. Make sure you use an equal amount of plasticine on both sides of the pencil, or the arrow won't balance properly.

7. Use cellophane tape to fix one paper clip over the hole in the stand. Fix the other one to the base, directly underneath. Stand the pencil in the hole.
8. Mark the points of the compass on the base. Outside, point the base so that "E" faces the direction of the rising sun. Record the direction of the wind each day.

Record wind speed

To see how fast or slow the wind blows, make an *anemometer* – a wind speed measurer.
You will need **stiff cardboard** 24 inches by 12 inches.
1. Measure four 6 inch widths with a **ruler,** and draw **pencil** lines across these points.
Score down the lines with **scissors.**
2. Set a **compass** to 4 inches and draw an arc on the cardboard as shown.
Cut out a narrow slot along the arc.
Mark numbers at equal intervals along the slot.
Fold the cardboard inward along the scored lines. Put **cellophane tape** along the two edges and along all the folded edges.
3. Cut a piece of **paper** 4¾ inches square and tape it to the end of the box as shown.
Take the anemometer outside and point the flap toward the wind. Each night and morning, record the level that the flap reaches.

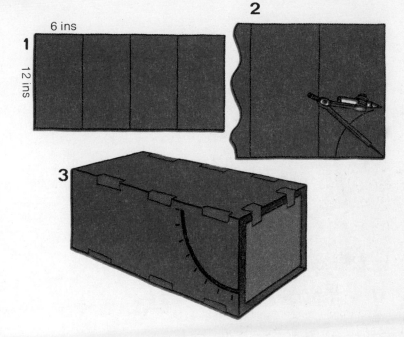

Measure the rain

Keep a record of the amount of rain that falls by using a simple measuring device.
Find **four empty glass jars.** They must have straight sides and all be the same size.
Put the jars outside and wait for it to rain.
Let the jars collect water over a 24-hour period.

Now pour all the water you've collected into just *one* of the jars.
Use a **ruler** to measure the water's depth. Divide the depth by the number of jars. For instance, if the water measures 2 inches the sum will be $\frac{2}{4}$ (or $\frac{1}{2}$), which means that $\frac{1}{2}$ inch of rain has fallen.

Consequences

In this game nobody wins or loses but everyone will laugh when it is finished. Two or more people can play the game.

Each player needs **paper** and a **pencil**.
1. At the top of the paper each player draws the head of a person or animal. The head must have a long neck drawn on it.

2. Each player folds over the paper so that only the neck shows. Then the folded paper is passed on to the next player.

Five stones

This is a game to play when you're all by yourself and you want to amuse yourself.

Five Stones is an old game, and there are many ways to play it. The Ancient Greeks played it with the ankle bones of sheep.
You need **five stones** (obviously!) but practice with three until you are good at the game.

Put the five (or three) stones in the palm of your hand.
Throw the stones into the air. Now, turn your hand over, spread your fingers as wide as possible, and try to catch all the stones on the back of your hand as they fall.

Or hold one stone in your hand and put the other four on the ground. Throw the one stone into the air and, before catching it, pick up one stone from the ground. Do the same, trying to pick up two stones, then three, then all four.

3. Without looking under the fold, each player adds a body to the neck. It can be lifelike or funny or silly.
The papers are folded and passed on again.

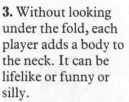

4. Finally, draw legs and feet, and pass on the papers as before. Now unfold the papers. Who's got the funniest or strangest "human-animal"? Can anyone give it a name?

Pick-up-sticks

Toy stores usually sell special sticks for playing this game but ordinary **lollipop and ice cream sticks** work just as well.

Ask all your friends to save their lollipop and ice cream sticks for you. Wash the sticks and let them dry. You will need about 30. Play the game on your own, or challenge one of your friends to play with you.

Each player chooses one stick as a "playing stick".
The rest of the sticks are held in an upright bunch by one player. This player then lets all the sticks fall in a heap on the floor or table.

The first player uses his or her playing stick to lift one stick from the heap. The player must not make any other stick move. If he or she does, then it's the other player's turn. The player who lifts off the most sticks is the winner.

A friendly file

The police keep records of photographs and fingerprints to identify people. Here's an "identity" file with a cheerful difference: a collection of lip and fingerprints on cards. Ask your friends and family if they would like to be included in your special file. Then make cards all the same size by cutting up **thin cardboard** with **scissors.** Use a **pencil or pen** to write in a person's name, address, birthday, color of hair and eyes, height and weight, or hobbies. Paste on a photograph if you have one. Ask someone to lend you an **old lipstick.** Rub the lipstick on a friend's finger and press the finger firmly on that person's card. Do the same with lips and ask everyone to "kiss" their personal card.

For a file, use a **box or ribbon.** Punch a hole in each card to thread ribbon through.

Alphabet letters

Have you ever noticed how many different kinds of **letters** there are? Look at the variety of letters printed in books, magazines and newspapers or on advertisements, labels and greeting cards. Each kind of letter has its own name. For instance, the ordinary upright type – like the words printed here – is called roman. Slanting type (*like this*) is called italic.

Use **scissors** to cut out letters. (*Don't cut up books.*) Find as many different A's, B's and so on, as possible, and use **glue** to fix them in a **scrapbook.** You could have a page for each letter of the alphabet.

Or glue down your letters so that they make pictures. You could use them to design animals like this one, or houses, or people.

Money, money, money

Collect coins instead of spending them! Save up your own money or go on a treasure hunt for lost coins. (Make sure the coins you find don't belong to someone else.) Search under chair cushions, between floorboards, or behind dusty shelves. Ask traveling friends or relatives for their spare foreign coins.

If the coins you find are dirty, wash them in **warm, soapy water** or soak them in a solution of **salt and vinegar.** Don't use metal polish to clean them as this will wear away the design. You could display your favorite coins in a special clay box. Cover them with plastic if you like. If you have extra coins, why not make a money paperweight?

Display box

1. Use a **rolling pin** to roll some **self-hardening clay** into a square or oblong shape. The clay should be about ¾ inch thick.

2. Make sure the top is very flat and even, then trim the edges of the clay with an **old kitchen knife** so that they are neat.

3. Press the **coins** into the clay until they are even with the top of it. Then carefully lift all the coins out.

4. Let the clay harden. Don't put it in a warm place or it will curl up. When the clay is hard, arrange your coins for display.

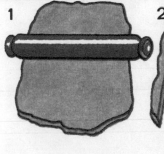

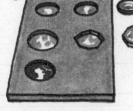

1

2

3

4

Coin paperweight

1. Pile up a handful of **coins.** Choose the sort that you have two or more of in your collection.

2. Use **scissors** to cut a piece of **stiff cardboard** into a base for your paperweight. It can be any shape.

3. Cover the top of the cardboard with **household cement,** and press down a layer of coins very close together.

4. Cement on more coins to make a pile. Trim off any cardboard that shows. Put **varnish** on the coins with a **brush.**

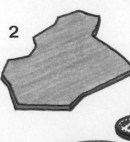

1

2

3

4

Count the cats

Can you see cats in this picture ? Altogether there are 25 – some are huge and some are very tiny and a few are upside down.

The tricky T

Use **pencil** to trace these shapes onto **tracing paper,** then use the pattern and **scissors** to cut out the shapes in **cardboard.** Number them, and keep all the numbered sides facing you.

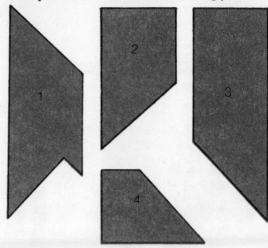

The four pieces fit together in a certain way to make a capital "T." See if you can do it.

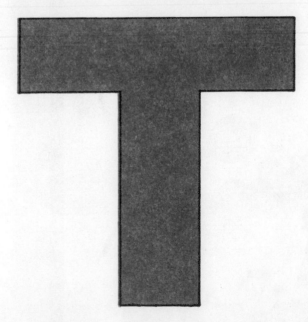

This "T" is exactly the same size as the puzzle pieces when they're put together properly. (The solution is in the back of the book.)

Solve the problem

A man is going to the market to sell a fox, a hen and some grain. He has to cross a river and his boat is just big enough to hold himself and one other thing.

When he gets to the river he finds he has a problem. If he leaves the fox with the hen, the hen will be eaten by the fox. He can't leave the hen and the grain together, because the hen will feast itself on the grain. Only the fox and the grain can be left safely together. How does the man get all three and himself across the river?

(You might have to think for a long time about this problem. Check your solution by looking at the pages of Answers in the back of the book.)

From one to nine

In these boxes the numbers placed diagonally (2,5,8) add up to 15. Can you arrange the rest of the numbers between one and nine (1,3,4,6,7, 9) so that the numbers add up to 15 in every direction? Add up all the rows of numbers from left to right and from top to bottom and the other diagonal row.

(Look in the back of the book for the answer.)

Finger pictures

Here's a clever way of making pictures without using crayons or brushes.
Pour some **poster paint** onto a **sponge.** Mix it with a little **water** if necessary, but do not make it too runny.

Press your finger first onto the sponge and then onto a clean sheet of **paper.** Experiment with your other fingers, the side of your hand or even your whole hand to make all kinds of pictures.

Here are some shapes to try:

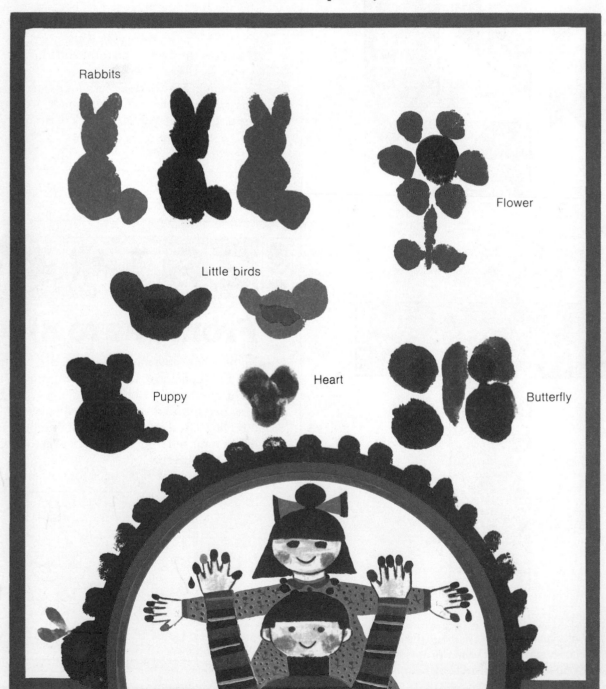

Rabbits

Flower

Little birds

Puppy

Heart

Butterfly

Magazine collage

Look through some **old magazines** and rip out the patches of plain color. Sort out the different colors into piles. Tear or cut up the pieces of paper as you use them.

Use **glue** to stick the pieces down on a sheet of **paper** to make a picture. Think how you can use light and dark shades of the same color. Use dark shades for shadows, for instance.

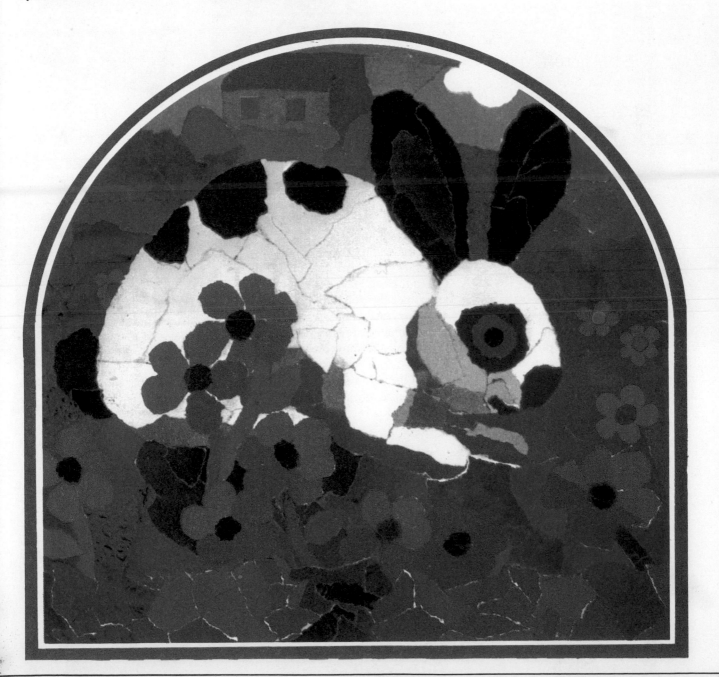

Predict the card

This special bag will help you "predict" which card will be chosen from a whole **deck of cards**.

1. Use **cellophane tape** to fix a **sheet of paper** into a **paper bag** so that it makes two compartments.

2. Put a playing card in one side of the bag. With a **pencil,** write the name of the card on **a slip of paper.** Put it in the same compartment.

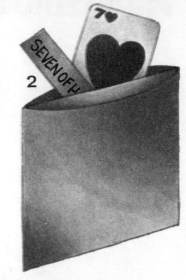

★ ★ ★ ★ ★ ★ ★ ★ ★ ★ ★ ★ **Performance** ★ ★ ★ ★ ★ ★ ★ ★ ★ ★ ★ ★ ★

Show everyone the "ordinary" bag.

3. Pretend to write the name of a card on **another slip of paper.** Put the slip into the *empty* compartment of the paper bag.

4. Spread all the cards face down and ask someone to touch any card.

5. Put the touched card into the same compartment of the bag as the blank paper slip.
Hold the secret divider against the other side of the bag.

6. Tip the bag up so that the card and paper slip you put in secretly will drop out.

7. Ask someone to read your prediction and show the card. They will be a perfect match! (Don't let anyone see that there is still a card and slip of paper in the bag.)

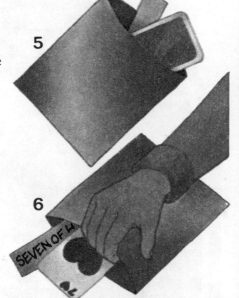

SEVEN OF H

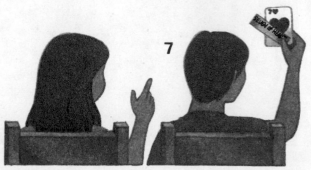

Robot ball

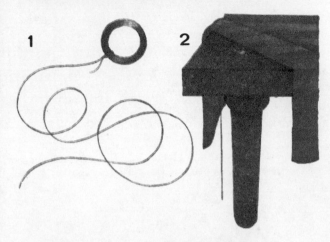

1

2

Ask a friend to help you do this magic trick.
1. Tie a long piece of **cotton thread** to a **curtain ring.**
Put the ring on a **table** with the thread hanging over the edge.
2. Cover the table with a **cloth.**

Performance

Tell your audience you can command a ball to move of its own accord.
Put a **small ball** on the hidden ring.
3. At your command, your friend pulls the thread hanging under the tablecloth.
The ball will then roll across the table.

3

Scratch it out

Here is a different trick of movement that will surprise your friends.
Put **two big coins** on a **tablecloth,** then put a **smaller coin** between them.
1. Turn a **glass** upside down so that its rim rests on the two big coins.
Ask someone to try to get the smaller coin out without touching the glass or any of the coins.
When the person gives up, you can show how easily it is done.
2. Keep scratching the tablecloth in front of the glass. Gradually, the smaller coin will move out from under the glass.

1

2

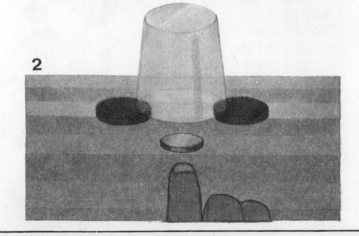

Take a peek!

Imagine being able to watch wild animals eating or sleeping or playing right before your eyes. It's very difficult to do this out-of-doors, but you can observe animals any time you like through the glass wall of a *vivarium*. Vivarium is the proper word for a container in which you raise small animals in surroundings where they feel at home. Use a fish tank or **ask an adult** to help you make a vivarium out of a box. You will need a **strong wooden box** 24 inches long, 20 inches wide, and 20 inches deep. Look for a box in secondhand or junk shops, or **ask an adult** to build one for you with a base and three sides. Make sure there are no gaps in your box.

Buy from a hardware store: 64 inches of **plastic track;** a piece of **glass** $\frac{1}{4}$ inch by $23\frac{3}{4}$ inches by $19\frac{3}{4}$ inches; two pieces of **pine** 24 inches long and 1 inch wide and two more pieces 18 inches long by 1 inch; **nails; four corrugated fasteners;** a tube of **wood glue;** a piece of **wire mesh** 24 inches by 20 inches; a box of **staples;** a piece of **plastic or polyethylene** 26 inches by 22 inches; **paint** and a **paintbrush.** You will also need **soil.**

1. Take off one long side of the box by knocking against it with a **hammer.** Put several coats of paint on the inside. Let the paint dry.
2. Cut the plastic track in three pieces to fit along the open sides and nail in place. Slot the glass into it.
3. Glue the pieces of pine together as a frame for the top.

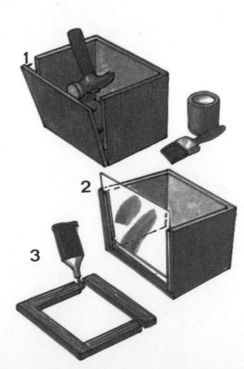

4. Hammer a corrugated fastener across each joint of the frame to hold it firmly.
5. Stretch the wire mesh over the frame and fix it into place with staples.
6. Line the floor with the plastic or polyethylene so that an inch or so is turned up against the side of the box to hold the soil.

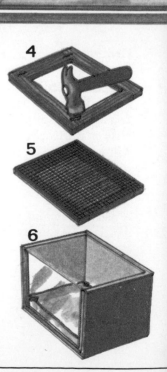

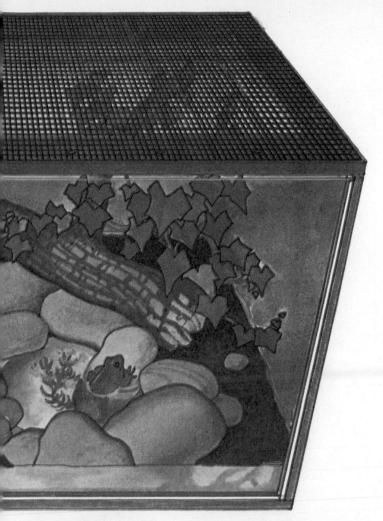

Choosing an animal

You could raise frogs and toads in the vivarium, or lizards. Pet shops sell all these. Read some books about the conditions and food an animal likes before you decide to raise one.

Decorating the animal's home

Look at the chart below to see what kind of **soil, plants** and other things you should put into the vivarium for the animal you have chosen. You can make a pond by sinking a **bowl** into the soil, then filling it with **water**.
Slope the soil away from the pond and surround it with **stones**. Put plants directly into the soil, or grow them in pots and then sink these into the soil. Plants should be growing well before you put an animal into the vivarium.

Catching the food

Look under stones or logs in your garden, or in woods and parks for worms. Catch insects in a butterfly net (Project 132). Sweep the net through bushes and undergrowth to catch them. Because there are different *species* (or types) of animals, you may have to experiment with food to see which sort your animal likes best. Always make sure the pond has fresh water all the time.

Animals	Soil	Plants	Conditions	Food
Frogs and toads	Moist soil mixed with peat.	Split-leaf philodendron and pond weeds.	Small pond with rock in it for sitting on. Keep the vivarium in a shady place all the time.	All insects; worms and mealworms. Feed once or twice a week.
Lizards	Dry soil mixed with gravel and sand.	A sedum plant and ivy. Dry fern or heather to scratch dead skin against.	Rocks; sticks or branches. Put the vivarium in a warm spot for a few hours each day.	Live insects. Feed about twice a week.

Sausages

The faster you play this game and the more people playing it, the funnier it is.

Choose one player to be "It."
All the other players take turns asking It a question. Ask anything you wish – it could be "What's your name?", "Who is your best friend?" or "What is your teacher like?" Whatever the question, It must always answer "Sausages!" – without laughing.
If It laughs, he or she is out and someone else is chosen to be It.
You'll probably find that nobody (including It) can stop laughing!

Slowpoke

Think like a snail because in this race the player who comes in last is the winner!

Mark out a short distance for the racetrack. Line all the players up on the track. When the starter says "Go!" everyone moves off as *slowly* as possible. Anyone who stops completely is out. The last player across the finishing line wins.

Sniffies

Next time you have a party, play this game with all your guests. Identifying things by smell is not easy, but it's amusing to try. See how many correct guesses everyone makes.

You need a **pencil, paper** and a **blindfold** for each guest, **four saucers** and **four things to sniff.**
Choose things with a strong smell – curry powder, cocoa, coffee, lemon peel or dish washing liquid. (**Ask an adult** for these things.)
Put one thing in each saucer secretly.
Blindfold all the guests and bring in the saucers. Warn them to sniff *gently*, then each player takes a turn sniffing. Then take all the saucers away, and ask the players to write down their four guesses.
The player with the most correct answers wins.

You can play a different version of this game by trying to identify things by the way they *feel*.
All the players must be blindfolded. A **few objects** are put into an **old pillowcase or sack.** These could be a feather, a piece of rubber, something wooly or silky, a scrap of felt or a piece of fruit such as a banana or an apple.
Everyone plays the game as "Sniffies" is played, except they feel instead of smell.

Guess how I do it

This is an acting and guessing game. You don't need to be a good actor and your guesses might be wild ones, but the game is fun to play. Two people or a whole group can play it.

One player is chosen to leave the room. He or she is the guesser.

The others pick an *adverb* (a word describing how something is done). It might be "angrily," "cunningly," "stupidly," or some other word. When everyone is ready, the guesser comes in and commands one of the players to act the word by performing a task. He or she might say, "Brush your teeth" or "Walk across the room." The player must do whatever the guesser asks in a way that describes the chosen word.

If the guesser can't tell what the word is, he or she can ask another player to act a different task. When the guesser gets the right answer, somebody else becomes the guesser, and another word is chosen by the rest of the players.

Interruptions

Ask someone in your family to play a word game with you if a rainy day keeps you all indoors.

You will need a **newspaper or a magazine.** Decide to be someone who sells things – say, a grocer, a butcher, or a candy store owner. Your partner has to read from the newspaper or magazine, skipping all the *nouns* (the words that name things). Whenever there is a pause, you call out the name of something you sell. The most boring piece of news suddenly becomes very funny when you fill it with "bananas" or "pig's feet" and so on!

Constantinople

Here is another word game you can save for a wintry or rainy day.

You will need **pencils, paper, a clock** and two or more players.

Choose a long word – one with at least ten letters in it. (Look in a **dictionary** or ask an adult if you can't think of one.)

Each player writes down smaller words, using any of the letters in the long word. The words must not be *proper nouns* (names of people or places) and they should have three or more letters in them. (Check words in a dictionary.) The player with the most words wins.

Now, go! You have five minutes to play.

String telephone

Call a friend on a homemade telephone.
Cut two strips of **paper,** each 30 inches by
4 inches.
1. Roll each strip into a cylinder 4 inches in
diameter. Fix the seams with **cellophane tape.**
Put each cylinder on **cardboard** 8 inches by
4 inches.
2. Draw around the cylinders with a **pencil,** and
use **scissors** to cut out the two circles.
Make a small hole in the center of each circle.
3. Tape one circle to the end of each cylinder.
4. Thread one end of a long piece of **string**
through each hole. Tie big knots in the ends.
Keep the string taut when you "telephone ."

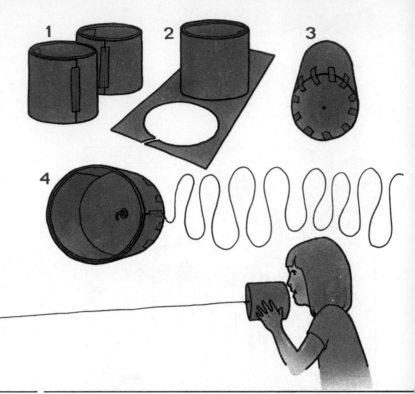

Magnet racetrack

See how magnets work (they attract most metal
objects containing iron) and have fun, too.
1. Using **scissors,** cut out the bottom and sides
of a **box** as shown.
Cut two 1½ inch-wide **cardboard** strips longer
than the box. (Don't use really thick cardboard.)
2. Fix the strips to the box with **cellophane tape.**
Now you need **two rulers** and **two magnets.**
Put a lump of **plasticine** on the end of each ruler
and press a magnet into each lump.
Get **two paper clips** and put one on the end of
each track. A player must try to get his or her
paper clip to the end of the track by using the
force of the magnet. (Steady hands are needed!)
3. Hold the magnets below the tracks.
If your magnet touches the track or your
paper clip falls off, you must start again.

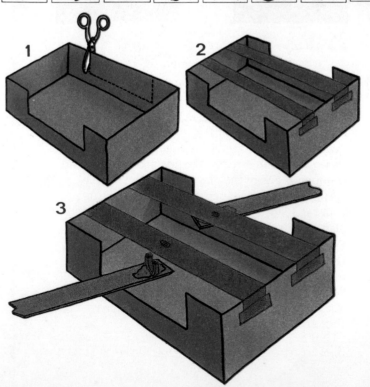

Stand-up clown

An eggshell will stand upright if you weight it. Dress it as a clown and watch it move!
1. Gently mold a lump of **plasticine** into the bottom of an **eggshell**.
Cut a strip of **paper** about 8 inches by 3 inches. Roll it into a cylinder the same size as the top of the shell. Join the edges with **cellophane tape**.
2. Tape the cylinder to the top of the shell. Use a **compass** to draw a 4 inch-diameter circle on paper. Cut it out with scissors.
3. Cut from the circle's edge to its center. Twist the circle into a cone shape and put cellophane tape on the seam.
Tape the cone to the paper cylinder to make a hat. Paint the clown with **poster paints**.

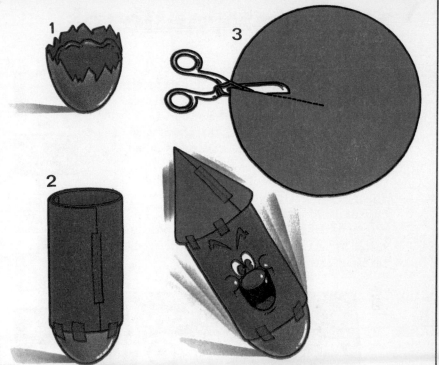

Soil settling jar

Soil is a mixture of different particles. It could include sand, clay, peat and gravel, though you may not be able to see them all. If you put soil into a **glass jar with a lid**, you will be able to see the different parts.
Use an **old spoon** to dig up a little **soil** from various places in a garden.
1. Half fill the jar with the different soils.
2. Fill the jar with **water**. Screw on the lid. Shake the jar well, and then let it stand. The soil will separate into layers – the heaviest part of the soil will settle on the bottom and the lightest will rest on top.

Going international

Modern postcards are easy to collect because they are sold all over the world. Buy them when you are on vacation or ask friends and relatives to send you postcards if they go on a trip. There are thousands of cards that show views of places or buildings. But there are many other kinds, too. You could look for postcards that show birds, animals or flowers, or ones that illustrate a joke. Or collect postcards of famous paintings from art galleries and museums. If you decide to collect old postcards, search in junk shops and secondhand bookshops for really cheap ones.

There are lots of ways to display postcards.
1. Arrange them on the floor in a long row, face down. Use **glue** to fix **postcards** to a length of **wide ribbon.**
With **thumbtacks,** fix the end of the ribbon to your bedroom door or to the wall.
2. Decorate a **tabletop** with a collage of **postcards.** They will stay in place if you cover them with a sheet of **glass. Ask an adult** to help you get glass cut to the right size.
3. Keep your **postcards** in a traditional **album.** Mount them with **transparent photographic hinges** so that you can see every bit of each card.

2

3

Postcard cubes
Cut a piece of **paper** 16 inches by 12 inches.
1. With a **pencil** and **ruler,** draw on it six squares, each measuring

$3\frac{1}{2}$ inches, and seven tabs as shown. Use **scissors** to cut up **postcards** into $3\frac{1}{2}$ inch squares.
2. Glue the postcard squares to the paper squares.

When the **glue** is dry, fold the paper into a cube.
3. Spread glue on the tabs and stick them together.

1
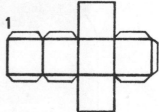

2
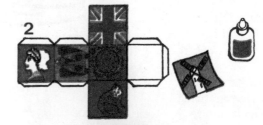

3
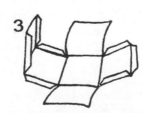

Make as many cubes as you like by repeating steps 1-3.
Pile the cubes up to make an attractive group of pictures.

When your pile topples over, give your extra cubes away as Christmas or birthday presents.

As sweet as sugar

When you go to a restaurant or lunchroom, look out for **wrapped-up sugar cubes or** little **printed packets of sugar.** Ask the waiter or the owner if you can have some for your collection. You might also see specially-wrapped sugar at airports or in hotels and theaters.

Sugar jar
There are lots of different designs on wrappers and packets. Collect as many as you can, and fill up a **big glass jar** with wrapped sugar.

Wrapper diary
Use **glue** to stick **empty wrappers** into a **diary or notebook.** With a **pencil or pen,** write next to each one the place where you collected it, the date, who went with you, what you ate, and if anything special happened.

Beads all in a row

Beads are lovely things to collect because they come in so many different colors, materials, shapes and sizes. Ask your mother (or an aunt or grandmother) if she has any beads from a broken necklace. Or buy beads in thrift shops, craft and hobby shops or rummage sales. You could collect glass beads or wooden ones, or beads of all kinds. String them on a length of thin cord to make a necklace. Or **ask an adult** to help you display them in a frame.

Bead picture
1. Use a **hammer** to put **nails** into the sides of an **old picture frame.** Space them evenly on both sides and leave the heads sticking up a bit.

Tie a piece of **thin string** to one nail.
2. Thread **beads** on it, and tie the end of the string to the opposite nail. Dab the knots with **household cement.**

3. Continue threading beads on lengths of string for each pair of nails.
Hang the frame on your bedroom wall for everyone to admire.

Which way to go?

Imagine you are walking down a road from a little town. You're on your way to visit someone in another town.

After a mile or so, you reach a crossroad. Here there should be a signpost pointing in all four directions, naming the town at the end of each of the four roads. The signpost is there, but it has fallen over. Its four pointers are still attached to it.

How do you know which road to take? There is no one to ask and you can't see any of the towns in the distance.

(There is a very simple solution, and it is given in the back of the book.)

Two-way envelope

Can you draw this envelope without taking your **pencil** off the **paper**? The only rule is that you must not go back along any line you've already drawn.

A clue: there are two places where you could start drawing, so there are two solutions to this puzzle.

(The answers are in the back of the book.)

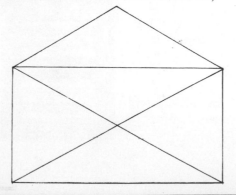

Odds and evens

Some of the cars in this picture are identical in everything except color. But some are odd because they don't match any other car.

Count up the pairs that match each other. How many odd ones are left?
(The answer is in the back of the book.)

Korshinodoniger

This weird creature with the imaginary name is made up of parts of six real animals. See if you can identify each one of them.
(All six animals are listed on the pages of Answers in the back of the book.)

Lots of triangles

There are 35 triangles in this *pentagon* (five-sided figure). Can you find them all?
(Look in the back of the book for the answer.)

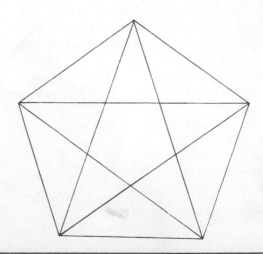

Squirmy wormery

Worms live underground where you can't see, but you can watch them at home in a wormery.
Find a **large empty jar.** You won't need a lid.
Put in a layer of **damp soil.** Add a layer of **sand.**
Then fill the jar with more damp soil.
With a **spade,** dig up a patch of earth to find **two or three worms.** Collect a **few leaves,** too.
1. Put the worms and leaves on top of the soil. Stretch a piece of **cheesecloth** over the jar and hold it in place with a **rubber band.**
2. Wrap **black paper** around the jar and fix the seams with **cellophane tape.**
Leave the jar for a few days.
3. Take the paper off. See how the burrowing worms have mingled the soil and sand?
To keep worms as pets, make sure that they always have fresh leaves and moist soil.

Fruit fancy

Here's a way to make sure that everyone knows which fruit is yours – initial it.
Use **scissors** to cut out your initials from a sheet of **black paper.**
Mix **flour** and **water** in a **bowl** to make a paste.
Put some paste on one side of the initials and stick them to a piece of **unripe fruit** – for instance, a green apple, a plum or a pear.
Leave the fruit in a sunny place to ripen.
Remove the paper when the fruit is ripe.
Wash off the paste and see your pale initials in the fruit.
(You can also initial tomatoes if you like.)

Grass shrieker

There are hundreds of different kinds of grasses. Some are grown by farmers and others grow wild in meadows, ditches, marshland, and even by the seashore.
Try making a shrieking noise with a **blade of grass.** Any kind of grass will do.
Turn the blade so that the edge of the grass is facing toward you.
Hold one end of the grass lengthwise between your thumbs.
Hold the other end of it between the *heels* (or the bottom parts) of your hands.
Your hands should be cupped around the grass and the blade should be stretched tightly.
Now blow across the blade of grass and listen to the shrieking sound you make.

Egging you on

You can make interesting and unusual egg decorations once you know how to hollow out eggs. (Always save the inside of the egg so someone can cook it later.)
Put an **egg** in an **eggcup**.
1. Gently pierce a hole in one end with a **darning needle**.
Pierce another hole, a little larger, in the other end.
2. Hold the egg over a **bowl** and gently blow into the smaller hole until all the egg comes out at the other end.
Carefully run water through the egg to clean it thoroughly, and then shake it dry.

3. Coat half the egg with **white glue**.
4. Stick on **braid, yarn and tiny beads or seeds**.
Let the glue dry.
Turn the egg and decorate the other half the same way.

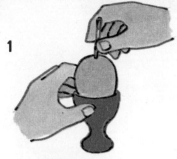
1

2 3 4

Pebble pot

Look for some **fine gravel or little pebbles**.
1. Coat the outside of the **flowerpot** up to the rim with **household cement**. Also coat one side of the pebbles with cement.
2. When cement is tacky, press on pebbles in any pattern you like. Let the cement dry.

1 2

Burr babies

Burrs are the tiny rough seeds of plants such as wild carrot and burdock. They stick to the fur or feathers of animals or birds and they stick to your clothes as well!
In the summer you could collect a paper bag full of **burrs** from fields and meadows.
Try making some models by sticking the burrs to each other.
Use one burr for a doll's head, then stick a lot of burrs together to make a body.
Make animals in the same way.
Or make a shallow burr basket. Stick burrs together to make a bottom. Then shape curved sides out of burrs. If you like, put a small dish of water in the basket and fill it with pretty flowers.

Mind-reading ribbons

This trick should convince your friends that you have some very magical ribbons!

1. Use **small rubber bands** to join **three differently-colored ribbons** into a circle.

2. Put the ribbon circle into a **paper bag.**

You will need **three more ribbons** the same colors as the ones fastened together.

1

2

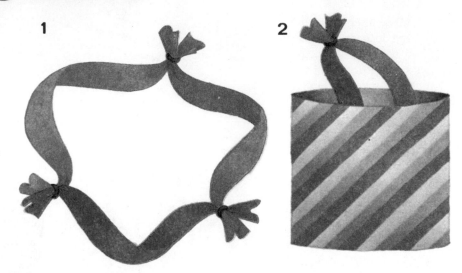

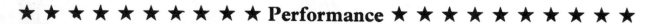 ★ ★ ★ ★ ★ ★ ★ ★ ★ ★ ★ **Performance** ★ ★ ★ ★ ★ ★ ★ ★ ★ ★ ★ ★

Give the three spare ribbons to someone in your audience.

3. Ask the person to tie them into a long strip, but not to let you see it.

Show everyone the paper bag. Tell them it holds three ribbons which are able to tie themselves into the same order as the spare strip of ribbons.

4. Ask the person with the spare ribbons to hold up the strip. Look at the colors showing at the top and bottom of the strip. (You must remember what the colors are.)

3

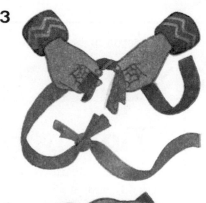

4

Dip into the bag and slip off the rubber band that joins the two colors you noticed in the strip.

5. Take hold of the same color as the other person is holding, and draw the ribbons from the bag. The order of colors will be the same!

5

Color jump

This trick works almost by itself.
1. Put a sheet of **red paper** on top of a sheet of **yellow paper**, allowing a 2 inch overlap.

1

2. Roll the papers up almost to the end of the red sheet of paper.
When you have reached the end of the yellow sheet it will flip right over.

2

3. Now unroll the papers and the yellow one will be on top.

3

Double six

Here's a way to throw sixes every time.
1. Use **household cement** to fix **two dice**, sixes up, into one end of a **large matchbox** drawer.

1

2. Drop **two spare dice** into the other end of the drawer and close the box.

2

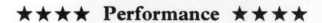

★★★★ Performance ★★★★

Open the box a little and tip out the loose dice. Ask someone to drop them back into the box.
3. Shake the box and say you will throw sixes.

3

Keep the box tilted slightly so that the loose dice stay at one end of the drawer.
4. Open the box at the other end to reveal the two glued-down dice with sixes showing.

4

Pecking bird

This little bird will peck for food at the touch of your finger.

Find a **large plain cork,** a **smaller plastic-topped cork** and a **matchbox.**

Paint them all with **poster paint** and a **brush.**

Push **three plastic toothpicks** into the large cork to make the bird's legs and neck. Make sure the toothpicks fit tightly.

Push the plastic-topped cork onto the neck to make the head.

Add **half a toothpick** for the beak and **two map pins** for the eyes.

Find a **feather** for the tail. Make a hole for it with the other piece of toothpick.

Cut out wings from **felt or cardboard** and use **glue** to stick them to the body.

Turn the matchbox upside down and poke the bird's legs through the box and the drawer. Push the drawer slightly to and fro, and watch the bird peck away.

Soup can dragster

Ask an adult to help you make this racing car.
Squash the open end of an **empty soup can**.
Use a **hammer** and **nail** to punch four small
holes in the open end for the front axle.
Punch two larger holes at the other end. Make
the holes big enough to take ¼ **inch dowelling**.
For the wheels, find **two rimmed tin lids** and
two wooden balls with ¼ inch holes.
Paint them with **acrylic paint** and a **brush**.
Push a piece of dowel ¼ inch wider than the
can through the back axle holes.
Fix a piece of dowel 1½ inches wider than the can
to the front of the car by threading **wire** through
the holes. Twist the ends of the wire.
With **scissors**, cut a **cardboard** windshield.
Paint it and the car. Find a **plastic-topped
cork** and paint a face on it for the driver.
Use **household cement** to stick on the driver,
the windshield and both sets of wheels.
Add **two corks** for headlamps.

wiggle nail
to make
¼ inch hole

front
axle
holes

twist ends
of wire

The still coin

Everything has *inertia* (pronounced *in-ersha*). This means that everything needs a force to start it moving. Try this experiment to see that this is true.

1. Put a **small coin** in the middle of a sheet of **cardboard** about 3 inches square.
Close your hand to make a fist.
Balance the cardboard on the back of your fist.
2. Keeping your hand perfectly still, flick the cardboard away *very* quickly.
3. The coin will stay on your fist.

1

2

3

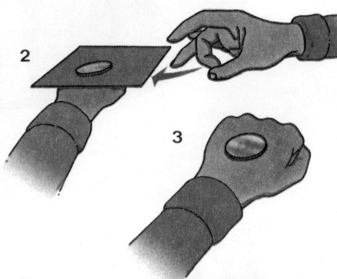

The coin can only be moved by an external force acting upon it. But when you flick *quickly* at the cardboard, very little of the force in your finger reaches the coin.
If you are in a car that starts suddenly, you feel your body being pressed back against the seat. Your body's inertia acts against the car's movement.

The moving coin

In this experiment you will see how a coin's *momentum* (or motion) keeps it moving.
Prop a piece of **cardboard** up at a slight angle to the floor.
Put a **small coin** on the roof of a **toy car.**
1. Let the car roll down the cardboard slope.
2. When the car stops slowly the coin will remain on the roof.

1   **2**

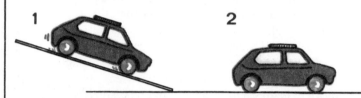

Now put a **thin book** a little way in front of the cardboard slope.
3. Roll the car (with its coin) down the slope.
4. The coin will shoot off the roof when the car stops suddenly against the book.

3   **4**

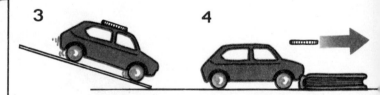

The book stops the car, but its force does not reach the coin so the coin's momentum keeps it moving. In the same way, if you are in a car that stops suddenly, your body's momentum will throw you forward. A seatbelt acts as a force to stop you and keep you safe.

Straight light

Light travels only in straight lines, but it is also reflected from objects. We can see the moon at night because the sun's light travels in a straight line to the moon and the moon reflects it in a straight line to earth. You can easily see for yourself how light travels.

Borrow a **flashlight** from someone. With **scissors,** cut a piece of **dark-colored paper** big enough to cover the bulb end of the flashlight. Fold the paper in half and cut a narrow slit in the middle. Fix the paper over the end of the flashlight with **cellophane tape.**

Put out all the lights in a room. Turn on the flashlight and point it at a **mirror.** The flashlight beam will be reflected so that it shines on the wall opposite the mirror.

Static balloon

A balloon will remain *static* (or at rest) on a wall if you give it an electrical charge. The amount of electricity is very low and won't hurt you. Blow up a **balloon** and tie the neck tightly. Gently rub the balloon on a piece of **soft clothing** such as a wooly sweater or a pair of nylon stockings.

Now press the balloon carefully against a **wall.** It will stay there for quite some time because the wall, which is uncharged, attracts the charged balloon. As the electrical charge wears down, the attraction is weakened and the balloon will fall off the wall.

Threading ice

This experiment shows that the freezing point of water is lower under pressure. Put an **ice cube** on a **tray.** Hold a piece of **strong wire** firmly in both hands and press it down on the ice cube. Press until the wire has gone halfway through. Now you can pick up the ice cube on the wire. The ice cube isn't cut in two because the pressure on the wire melts the ice. Once the wire has passed through, the melted ice re-freezes. (See Project 212 for a magic trick like this.)

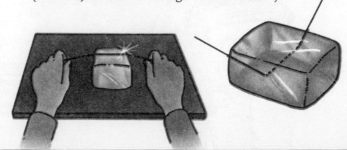

Blow soccer

Can you imagine a soccer game played on an ordinary table? This is soccer with a difference! It is easy to play and a lot of fun.

At each end of a **large table,** arrange some **matchboxes** in a three-sided-box shape to act as the goals.
Put some things along the edge of the table to keep the ball from falling off – **more matchboxes or toy building bricks** will do.
The soccer game can be played either between two players or two teams.

You now need **drinking straws** for each of the players and one **table tennis ball.**
Decide which goal belongs to each player or team of players.
Put the ball in the center of the table.
At the word "Go!" the players on both sides try to get the ball into their opponents' goal.
(You must not touch the ball with your hands.)
Each time a goal is scored the ball is put back in the center of the table and the game starts again.
The player who scored has first blow.
If a player makes the ball roll off the table, his opponent puts the ball on the spot where it rolled off and re-starts the game.
The player with the most goals at the end of the time (say, ten minutes) is the winner.

Captain's treasure

This is a party game for playing indoors. It's very easy, but **ask an adult** which room you should play in before you start.
You need a **few small objects** as "treasure" – for instance, a thimble, a stamp, a piece of costume jewelry and a coin. Gather about ten objects in all.

One person is chosen as the treasure holder. All the other players divide into two teams and each team chooses a Captain.
Both teams leave the room while the treasure holder hides the objects in different places.
The teams come in and the treasure holder calls out the name of one of the objects.
Everyone must search for it, but when it is found only the Captain can touch it. He takes it to the treasure holder and his team scores one point.
The treasure holder names another object, and so the game goes on until all the objects have been found.
The team with the most "treasure" wins.

Gelatin shovel

If you like food and sometimes get very hungry, you're sure to enjoy this game.

Put on some **old clothes** and play this game outside because it's a bit messy.
For two players, you will need **two bowls of gelatin, two wooden spoons,** and **two blindfolds. (Ask an adult** before you raid the kitchen.) The players sit opposite each other with their blindfolds on.
Each player holds a bowl of gelatin in one hand and a spoon in the other.
They have to feed each other the gelatin. The first one with an empty bowl wins.

Score or bust

Here's a good indoor game for a rainy day. You can play it with one or more friends.

"Score or bust" is played with a **die** which each player throws once when it's his or her turn. A scorer has a **pencil** and **paper** and writes down the number thrown by each player every time. The idea is to score a total of 21 or as near to 21 as possible. If anyone scores over 21 he "busts" and is out of the game.
It doesn't matter how many turns each player has and players can skip a turn if they like.
The first player who scores 21 wins the game.
If no one can get 21, the player with the score closest to it is the winner.

Mapping your diet

Food and wine labels are very attractive. Have you ever noticed the variety of them in the kitchen cabinet? You could start a collection of labels from empty food cans, packages of cheese, bottles of wine, or from jars of preserves.
Soak bottles in **water** to remove their labels. Most labels on cans and boxes can be eased off if you are careful. (**Ask an adult** before you take cans or bottles from the kitchen.)

Labels often tell you where the food or drink came from and collecting them is an interesting way of learning about the world's produce. You could find out all about one or two countries at a time. You might have a label from some Polish ham, for instance, to go on a map of Poland; or from Edam cheese to put on a map of Holland; or from orange marmalade to go on a map of England.
Buy or draw **a map** of a country (or the whole world, if you like) and use **glue** to stick it to a large piece of **cardboard.** Leave room around the edges to add your labels.
With **scissors,** cut lengths of **thread.**
Tie the ends of the threads around **map pins.** Put one map pin in the area of the country for which you have a label. (If you have a world map put a pin in a particular country.) Stretch the thread beyond the map and fix the label to the cardboard with the other map pin.

A trim picture

Ask an adult if you can collect the **dress trimmings** from any old clothes or from finished sewing projects. Look for lace or crochet on cuffs and collars of blouses, sequins on dresses, ribbons and feathers on hats. You might even find some beautiful beadwork on an old evening dress. Use your prettiest pieces to make unusual cloth pictures or wall hangings.

Cover a piece of **stiff cardboard** with **white glue.** Stick down a **plain piece of cloth** on it. When the glue is dry, use **dressmaker's chalk** to draw a decorative shape on the cloth. You could draw freehand or trace a shape from a magazine. Glue all your trimmings within the outline to make a varied pattern.

Autographs

If you are interested in famous sports figures, pop stars or TV personalities you could make a hobby of collecting their *autographs* (or signatures). You could write to a famous person asking for an autograph. If you don't know his or her address, write "in care of" the sports arena, theater, record or film company where the person works and enclose a stamped, self-addressed envelope. If you write an interesting letter you may get a signed photograph or even a letter in return.

Keep an **autograph book** so that you can paste in your signatures with **glue.** You might be lucky enough to see a famous person in the street or in a restaurant, so carry your book and a **pen** with you when you go out.

Free your friend

Imagine that someone has imprisoned your best friend inside this castle. The castle is surrounded by a moat 3 yards wide.
You've come to rescue your friend but the two planks you have brought with you are only 2 yards, 33 inches long. Both planks are 3 inches too short and you have no way of attaching them together.
How can you arrange the two planks so that you are able to cross the moat?
(The answer is in the back of the book.)

Fishy problem

One of these fish is swimming in the wrong part of its sea circle. Can you see where it should be?
(The answer is in the back of the book.)

Mouse maze

This little mouse can see a tasty lump of cheese but it has to find its way through the pipes to get it. Can you help the little mouse?

Trace your path with your finger or put **tracing paper** over the page and use a **pencil.** (You'll find the route in the back of the book.)

Water pistols

Have fun out-of-doors with these pistols, but be sure to put on old clothes first.

Pull the squirter nozzles off **two empty dishwashing detergent bottles.** Wash the bottles inside and out. Let them dry.

1. Paint the bottles with **acrylic paints** and a **paintbrush.** Let the colors dry.

2. Fill the bottles with **water,** and replace the squirter nozzles.

Stand back-to-back with a friend, each of you holding a bottle pistol in both hands. Slowly walk three paces forward, turn and . . . squeeze!

Nailophone

Ask an adult to help you make an unusual musical instrument that plays in the breeze.

Buy a yard of **heavy galvanized wire** and **eight nails** about 3 inches long from a hardware store. From a plant shop or garden center buy a yard-long **bamboo** or **cane rod.**

1. Bend the wire into a snaky shape.

2. Tie a 14 inch length of **string** to each end of the wire and hang it from the rod.

Use **scissors** to cut eight pieces of **strong thread,** each 15½ inches long.

3. Tie one length of thread to each nail.

4. Hang the nails in a row along the rod so that their tips come just below the wire.

Use **more string** to tie the nailophone to a **tree branch or a window curtain rod.** When the wind blows, the nails will ping against the wire.

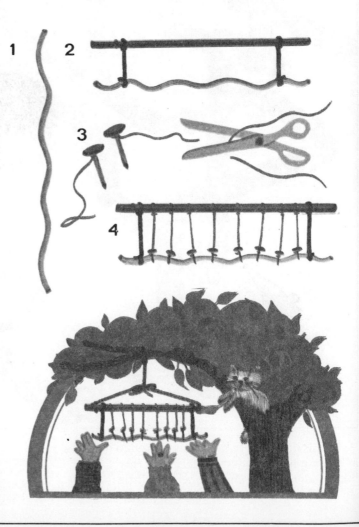

Party place mats

Colorful mats make a party table look festive.
Make some from **differently-colored papers.**
With a **ruler** and **pencil,** measure and mark ten
strips of paper each 13 inches by 1 inch.
1. Use **scissors** to cut out the strips.
In the same way, measure and cut eight more
strips of paper, each 16 inches by 1 inch.

Put the ten short strips side by side on a table.
Arrange the colors any way you like.
2. Starting half-way down the ten strips, weave
the eight longer strips in and out between the
shorter ones.
Leave about 1 inch at each edge of the mat.

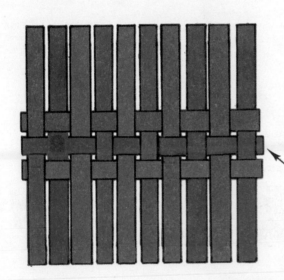

start weaving here
and work outward

fold over
and glue

3. Fold over the ends all around the mat and stick
them down with **glue.**
Make more mats in the same way.

Warming up

You need a few people in your audience to be able to do this magical trick.
Put several **coins** in a **box.**
Tell your audience that you can pick out a coin someone else chooses without seeing it first.
Ask someone to take out any coin while your back is turned.
Ask for the coin to be passed around so that everyone can look at it and remember it.
Then the coin must be put back in the box.
When you turn around, feel about in the box for the warmest coin and take it out.
Everyone will be amazed when they see that it is the right one.

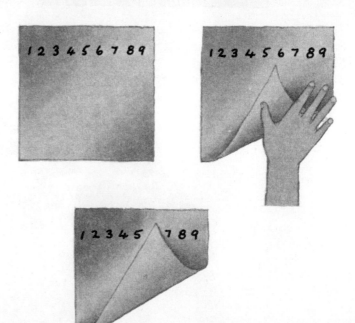

Vanishing number

This is a very cunning trick.
Tell your audience that you can make a number disappear from a sheet of paper.
Use a **pencil** to write the numbers between one and nine in a straight line along the top of a sheet of **paper.**
Ask someone to call out any number.
Fold up the bottom corner of the paper so that it covers the chosen number but leaves the other numbers visible.
Your audience will realize that it's a trick, but you have done what you said you could do!

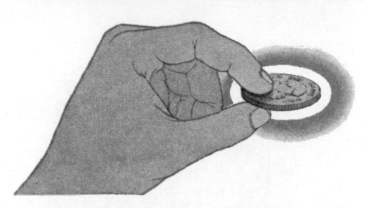

Adding master

Practice adding in your head, then copy these numbers in **pencil** onto five pieces of **cardboard**.

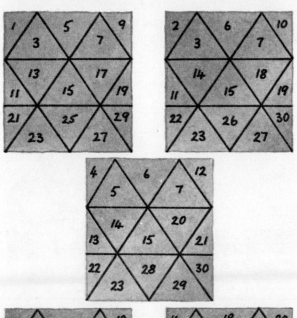

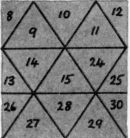
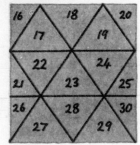

★★★★ **Performance** ★★★★

Give all the cards to someone and say you can name any number he or she secretly chooses simply by looking at the cards.

Ask the person to think of any number between one and 30 and to give you back all the cards that bear the chosen number.

In your head, add up the numbers in the *top left-hand corner* of each of the cards that have been handed to you.

Your total will be the chosen number.

X-ray eyes

Make believe that you have X-ray vision!
Cut two small **cardboard** circles with **scissors**.
1. Fix a **hair** to one with **cellophane tape,** then use **glue** to stick the cardboard circles together.
2. Cut three cardboard shapes as shown. Fold into pointed hats and tape the seams together.

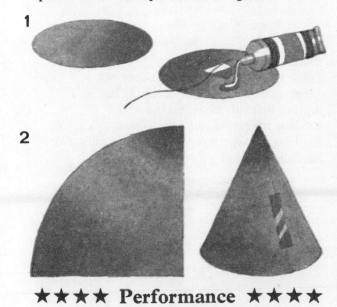

★★★★ **Performance** ★★★★

Ask someone to cover the circle with one hat while your back is turned.
When you turn around, look for the hair sticking out from under one of the hats.
Then you can say which hat hides the circle.

How time flies

Here's a way to make a **watch** (**or any small object**) disappear.
Use **glue** to stick the top of a **small paper bag** to the inside top of a **big paper bag**.

★★★★ Performance ★★★★

Show your audience the watch and say you can make it disappear.
1. Put the watch in the small paper bag.
(Everyone will think it is in the big bag.)
2. Blow up the big bag and burst it.
3. Show the empty torn bag. (The watch is still hidden in the small paper bag, but it will seem to have disappeared.)

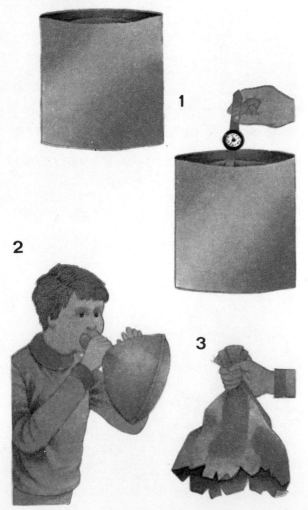

Turning point

This very easy trick works almost by itself.
Use a **felt-tipped pen** to draw an arrow on a small piece of **cardboard.**
Put the cardboard behind a **glass tumbler.**
Ask someone to look through the tumbler as you pour **water** into it.
When the tumbler is almost full the arrow will seem to turn and point in the other direction.

Great divide

Cut a strip of paper, yet leave it whole!
Cut two equal strips of **paper** with **scissors.**
1. Use **glue** to stick both pieces together, leaving a small unglued gap in the middle.
2. Fold one strip downward into a point at the middle, then fold the paper in half.

★★★★ Performance ★★★★

3. Hold the paper in your hand and cut right across the unglued fold.
Open out the strip and it will still be whole.

Big attraction

This trick makes your hand look magnetic.
Find a few **old playing cards.**
1. With **scissors,** cut a small square from one of the cards.
2. Fold the square in half and use **glue** to stick half of it to the back of another card.

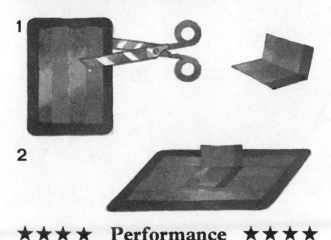

★★★★ Performance ★★★★

3. Put the special card, picture side facing upward, on the palm of your hand.
(You will find that you can hold the unglued part of the secret square between your fingers. Don't let anyone see the secret square.)
Use your other hand to slide more cards between the special card and your palm.
4. Carefully turn your palm over.
All the cards will seem to be sticking to your hand, just as nails stick to a magnet.

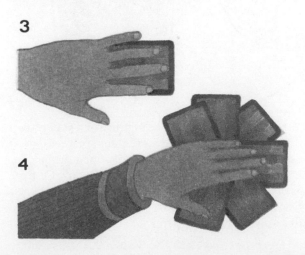

Shell garden

When you go to the seashore look among the rocks for **clam or scallop shells.** Make sure there are no creatures living inside them.
At home, wash the shells in **hot, soapy water.**
Use **tweezers** to pick out any bits left inside.
Rinse the shells in **clean water** and leave them on a **newspaper** to dry.
(If you like, you could varnish the outside of the shells with polyurethane varnish and a brush to make them shiny.)
Mount the shell in a small lump of **plasticine** so that it sits flat.
Fill the shell with **soil.**
Plant some **grass seed or miniature ivy** in the shell.

Variegated flower

Choose a **white flower** such as a chrysanthemum or carnation and change its color.
Slit the stem halfway up with a **kitchen knife.**
Put half the stem in **one glass tumbler,** half in **another.**
Put **water** in one tumbler.
In the other, put two teaspoons of **glycerine** and some **colored ink or food coloring.**
Watch the flower change color as it draws the dye up its stem.

Potpourri

A *potpourri* is a mixture of dried flower petals, leaves and spices. Gather lots of **flower petals** and **leaves** to make a pretty, perfumed mixture for your room. Choose scented flowers such as roses, jasmine, violets, narcissus and jonquils. Pick rose leaves and the leaves of basil, lavender, sage, marjoram or thyme. From a druggist buy a tiny package of **orrisroot powder** – this will help to preserve the color and scent of a potpourri for a long time.

1. Put the petals and leaves on **paper** in a dry, airy place out of direct sunlight. Turn them often until they are completely dry. Mix petals and leaves in a **bowl.** Try to get a good balance of color as well as the perfume you like best.

2. Add one **teaspoon** of orrisroot to every pint of mixture. Add the same amount of **spices** – cloves, allspice, or nutmeg for instance. Add a few drops of flower oils (from a druggist) if you like. Stir the mixture with a **spoon.**

3. Put the mixture in a **screw-top jar** and store it for six weeks. When it is ready, open the jar for a little while each day. Or tip the mixture into a bowl. The potpourri will lose its perfume more quickly, but it looks especially pretty this way.

Japanese lake

The Japanese regard ornamental gardens and
lakes as works of art – just like beautiful paintings
or fine poetry. The secret in making a miniature
Japanese lake is not to clutter it with too many
different things.

You will need a **shallow glass dish or bowl.**

1. Line the bottom with 1 inch of ordinary **soil**
and cover it with a layer of **gravel.**

2. Push a tiny piece of **driftwood or dried twigs**
into the soil and gravel.

Buy two or three **miniature water lilies** from a
florist or plant shop.

Plant the lilies in the soil and gravel.

3. Pour enough **water** into the bowl to just cover
the bottom of the lilies.

Keep adding water as the lilies grow.

Shell lady

Next time you go to the seashore, collect some
small shells. When you get home, wash off the
sand and use the shells to make a model.

First, shape a body out of **self-hardening clay.**
Roll a smooth ball of clay about the size of a
table tennis ball for the head. Make a cone shape
for the body.

1. Moisten the top of the triangle with **water** and
press the ball onto it.

2. To make arms, press in pointed shells.

3. Decorate the skirt with all sorts of the flatter
shells. Use a cup-shaped shell for a hat.

4. With **poster paints** and a **brush,** paint on
a nose, mouth and eyes.

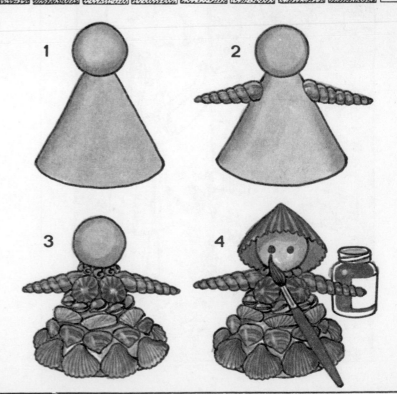

Seven-up

You can play this ball game on your own or with others players. It's called "Seven-up" because you have to catch a **ball** seven different ways in a certain order. You can make up the ways and their order yourself if you like, but here is a set of ways to start with:

1. Throw the ball against a **wall** and clap your hands once before catching it.

2. Throw the ball against a wall and clap twice before catching it.

3. Throw the ball against a wall and clap your hands over your head before catching it.

4. Throw the ball against a wall and spin around once before catching it.

5. Throw the ball against a wall and let it bounce under one leg before catching it.

6. Throw the ball against a wall and touch the ground before catching it.

7. Throw the ball against a wall and let it bounce on your head before catching it.

Hot potato

Persuade everyone to join in this musical game next time you have a party. You'll soon see that music and parties go very well together.

You will need **records** and a **record player or a radio** and a **small object** such as a bean bag or a soft toy. This is called the "hot potato."

All the players sit in a circle except one person who is in charge of the music.

When the music starts the hot potato is passed around the circle. When the music stops the player holding the potato must drop out.

The game goes on until there is a winner – only one person who has not held the hot potato.

Deep freeze

Play this game indoors or outside with either a few or lots of players.

Mark a starting line about 6 or 8 yards from a **wall (or a tree)**.

Choose one player to be It.

All the other players stand behind the starting line and It faces the wall.

The others have to try to creep up and touch It without being caught moving. If It turns around everyone must stop moving, or freeze on the spot. Anyone caught moving must go back to the start. The player who manages to touch It then faces the wall and play starts again.

Blindman's bluff

Older children will probably know this game well but here it is again for their younger brothers, sisters and friends to learn.

One player puts on a **blindfold.**

All the others dance around in a circle until the blindfolded person commands them to stop.

The blindfolded player points a finger and the player pointed to must come forward.

The blind person has to try to guess who it is by touch or by asking any question except "Who are you?"

If he or she guesses correctly the player who has been caught is blindfolded.

Otherwise the game continues until the blind person is able to identify someone.

Cops and robbers

When it's cold or wet outside ask a friend or someone in the family to play this indoor hunting game with you. All you need is an ordinary **checkerboard** and some **checkers.** Put four black checkers on the black squares at one end of the board. These are the "cops." Put one red checker on a red square at the other end of the board. This is the "robber." The robber has to try to reach the opposite end of the board. The cops have to try to box him or her in so that the robber cannot move. (There is no jumping over checkers in this game.)

The first move is made by one of the cops.

A cop can only move one space at a time, and only in one direction – forward.

The robber can move one space at a time in *any* direction, but only on the red squares.

Around the clock

The idea of this game is to throw all the numbers (one to 12) on a clockface using a **die.**

Someone with a **pencil** and **paper** keeps score. Taking turns, each player throws the die for one, then two, and so on up to six.

When a player has thrown a six he or she tries for one again to make seven, then for two to make eight, and so on until 12.

The first to throw "around the clock" wins.

Spool tank

This tank is powered by energy stored in a rubber band. (This is called *potential* energy.) Wind up the band and see what happens.

1. Use a **short pencil** to push a **rubber band** through an **empty spool.**

2. Hook one end of the rubber band over a **paper clip** and fix the clip to the spool with **cellophane tape.**

3. Push the other end of the rubber band through the hole in a **large washer.** Loop the end of the band over the pencil.

4. Turn the pencil around and around until the rubber band is twisted tightly.

Still holding the spool and pencil, put the tank on the floor. When you let go, the tank will race around the room.

Magnifying lens

When something is *magnified* it looks bigger. Water will act as a magnifier. Make this water-drop magnifying lens and see for yourself.

1. With a **pencil,** draw this shape on **stiff cardboard** 7 inches by $3\frac{1}{2}$ inches. Cut around the lines with **scissors.**

Cut a piece of **plastic** to fit the circular part.
2. Stretch the plastic over the hole and fix it with **cellophane tape.**

3. Put a **drop of water** on the plastic. Hold the lens over this page to magnify the words.

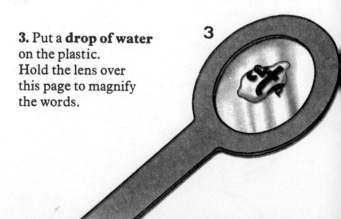

Light fader

Salty water is a conductor for the electricity that makes this toy work. The light fader can't possibly hurt you, but **ask an adult** to help because there are many steps to follow. Use the light in a toy theater or dollhouse.

From an electrical supply store buy: one **6 volt battery**, one **3½ volt bulb**, a **bulb holder**, and 6 feet of **thin electrical wire**.
Use **scissors** to cut the wire into two 14 inch-long pieces and one 1 yard-long piece.
1. Cut and strip off 1 inch of plastic covering from each end of all three pieces of wire.

1

2. Fix one short length of wire to each contact on the battery.
Screw the bulb into the bulb holder.

3. Fix the other end of one wire to one screw of the bulb holder.

4. Fix the long piece of wire to the other screw of the bulb holder.

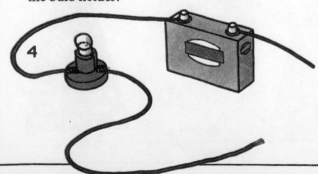

Now make *terminals* (the ends of the electrical circuit). You will need two piece of **aluminum foil, two paper clips** and **cellophane tape.**
5. Tape an opened-out paper clip to the two spare ends of wire.
6. Fold a piece of foil around each paper clip and bend up the spare paper.
Fill a **glass** with **water.** Add **salt,** stirring with a **spoon,** until no more salt will dissolve.

5    **6**

7. Bend the wire so that one foil terminal sits at the bottom of the glass.

7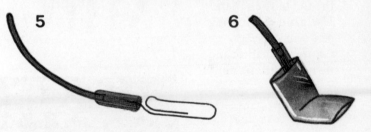

8. Put the other terminal into the water. You'll see the bulb get brighter as the terminals come closer together.

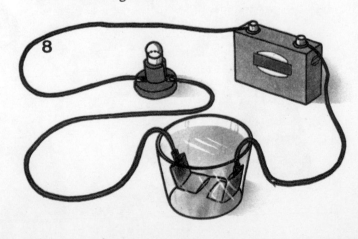

Clothespin doll

With a little patience you can turn a wooden clothespin into a pretty doll.

With a **ruler,** measure the height of a **wooden clothespin.**
Use **scissors** to cut out a square of **fabric** to the same measurement.

1. With a **needle** and **thread,** run a gathering stitch along the top of the square. Use **glue** to join the center back seam. Gather the fabric and tie it around the pin.

3. Paint a face on the doll with **acrylic paints** and a **brush.**

4. Glue on some short pieces of **yarn** to make soft hair.
Make a small **paper** triangle for the doll's kerchief.

2. Glue a piece of **ribbon** around the neck.

Make an impression

"How you've grown!" your mother will say when she sees a plaster print of your hand.

2. Remove your hand gently when you can take it away without taking plaster too.

Scratch your initials into the plaster with the wrong end of a **paintbrush**.

Mix **plaster of Paris** with **water** until it is smooth and stiff. Pour the plaster into a **foil pie pan.**

1. Press your hand into the plaster. Keep your hand still until you feel the plaster begin to set. Ask a friend to make a hand print, too, to keep you company.

Let the plaster dry completely.
3. Turn the plaster out of the dish and paint it with **acrylic or poster paint.**

Wax rubbings

You'll really begin to notice different designs if you take wax rubbings of things. A rubbing can be taken from anything which has an uneven surface. Find things around the house – wooden carvings, light switch plates, raised printing or designs on window glass and books, or textured wallpaper. Then have a look in your neighborhood for manhole covers, interesting bark on trees or brickwork on buildings.

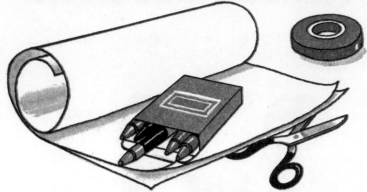

Use a **cloth** to dust the **uneven surface** you want to rub.
1. Put a sheet of **white paper** over it.
Fix the paper down with **masking tape.**

2. Rub slowly and carefully to and fro with a **wax crayon.** Make sure you rub in one direction only. You will soon see the pattern transferring itself to the paper.

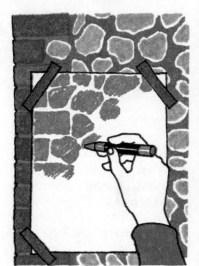

If you make a hobby of collecting different wax rubbings you may like to mount them in frames. To make a frame, cut a rectangle out of **stiff white or colored cardboard.**
1. Fold the rectangle in half.
2. Use **scissors** to cut a window in one side. (You could decorate the cardboard by painting it or by gluing on bits of lace.)
Trim your wax rubbing so that it is a little bigger than the window in the frame.
Use **glue** to stick the rubbing in position behind the window.
If you have sheets of rubbings left over you could use them as wrapping paper for presents.

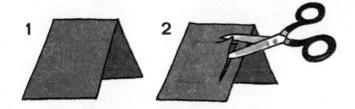

Bottle museum

You might see bottles in a real museum because some old ones are very valuable. Many modern **bottles** are also worth collecting for their beautiful shapes or for the unusual lettering pressed into the glass.

Ask your family and friends to save for you their empty perfume bottles, wine or liqueur bottles and old medicine jars.

Look for old bottles yourself in the shed or garage or on land where people throw their trash.

Watch out for bottles with decorations such as crests or seals impressed on them, for bottles with unusual necks or for ones made of colored glass.

Most bottles you find will probably be very dirty so soak them in **warm, soapy water** to clean them. Rinse the bottles in **clean water** and leave them on **newspaper** to dry.

Make a **cardboard** label for each bottle in your own museum. Use a **pen** to write in the date and place it was found or who gave it to you.

Fill up your bottles with colored stones or colored water, if you like.

Nail design

Nails differ in shape, size and color. Some have big heads, others have no heads at all; some nails are long and thick and others are tiny; some are steel-gray and a few are a golden copper color. See how many different kinds of **nails** you can find. Hunt for old nails in the garage and around the house. Or buy some new ones from a hardware store.

Ask an adult to help you display nails on a piece of **pine board**.

1. Use a **thick pencil** to draw an interesting design on the wood.

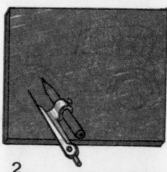

Work out where each nail goes in the wood.
2. Drive in the nails with a **hammer,** following the lines of the design.

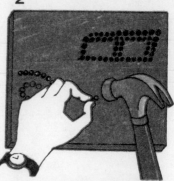

3. For variation, you could use **household cement** to fix some of the nails flat against the wood.

Cunning kitty

The order of events has been mixed up in this series of pictures. Can you sort it out? The top left-hand scene is the first in the series.
(The order is shown in the back of the book.)

AGFCBEDH

Ends to ends

How many bottles can you find in this picture?
(The answer is given in the back of the book.)

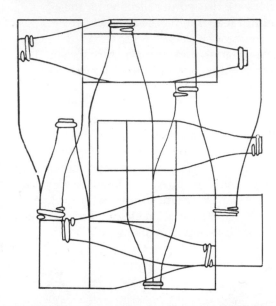

Load of problems

A man is driving a big interstate truck along a country road. He feels cheerful because he is on schedule. Suddenly he comes to a railroad bridge bearing a sign which reads: "Low bridge. Clearance 12 feet."
The driver stops in a hurry because he know his truck is exactly 12 feet, 1 inch high!
He gets out and thinks about the problem. The crates of goods are too heavy to lift off the truck and he doesn't want to make a detour because he will lose time. Eventually he works out a way to get the truck under the bridge. What does the driver do?
(The answer is given in the back of the book.)

Among the stars

This colored star is made up of five pieces. Can you find another star made up of only four?
Here's a clue: try holding the book away from you. (You can see where the star is in the back of the book.)

After-dinner gardens

The pits, seeds and stones from fresh raw fruit can be grown into new plants if you sow them in the spring. Try growing a lovely tree from an avocado pit. Then you could grow other plants from their seeds.

Avocado tree
Wash the **avocado pit** in water to clean it.
Let it dry.
1. Push **four toothpicks** into the pit about a third of the way up from the rounded end.

2. Rest the pit in a **jar** filled with **warm water** so that the round end sits in the liquid.
Leave the jar in a warm, dimly-lit place until the pit sprouts, or produces some roots.

3. Put some pebbles in the bottom of a **4 inch-deep flowerpot** and then fill the pot with **damp potting soil.**
4. Plant the avocado pit in the soil and leave it in a sunny place.
(Don't forget to water the avocado plant when the soil feels dry.)

A green display
Make the kitchen window-sill bright with other plants grown from seeds.
All **seeds** should be cleaned and dried first.
Don't forget to put **pebbles** in the **flowerpots** before adding **damp potting soil.**
Plant **one or two seeds** of a lemon or orange $\frac{3}{4}$ inch to $1\frac{1}{4}$ inches deep.
Plant just one seed in each pot for cherry, peach, plum, gourd or melon plants.
To grow tomatoes or peppers, plant two or three seeds to a pot. Then cover the pot with **glass** until the plants begin to sprout.
Make sure all your plants sit in a sunny spot.

Natural dyes

Dye your own T shirts with colors you have made yourself. **Ask an adult** to help you because the dye has to be boiled on a stove.
Here is a list of colors and the natural things that can produce them:

Pink or red
Beetroot; blackberries
Blue
Cornflowers; hollyhocks
Orange or tan
Onion skins; tea leaves
Yellow
Marigold petals; peach leaves
Green
Nettles; spinach
Brown
Walnut shells

Get as much **dyeing material** as possible. Put it in a **large saucepan** and cover it with plenty of **water.**
1. Boil it on the **stove** until you have a good strong color.

2. Pour the mixture through a **sieve.**
Add one tablespoon of **salt** to every quart of dye you have made.

3. Add an **old T shirt** to the dye and let it simmer on the stove for a few hours.
Rinse the T shirt in cold water until the dye stops coming out.
Hang it up to dry.

Your T shirt will look new again! Give the same treatment to faded cotton place mats or old cotton hats and handkerchiefs.

Flower power

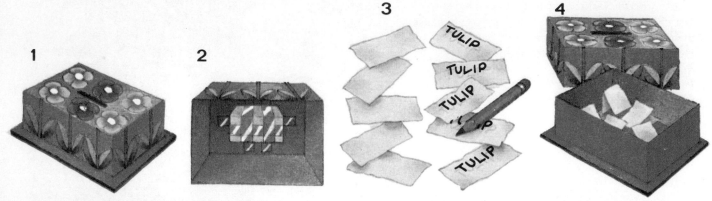

Prepare this special box and astonish your audience with your guessing ability.

1. Use **scissors** to cut a slot in the lid of a **big candy box.**

2. With **cellophane tape,** fix a **small open-topped box** under the slot of the big lid.

3. Cut twice as many small slips of **paper** as you will have spectators in your audience.
On half the slips write "tulip" in pencil.

4. Fold the slips in half and drop them into the bottom of the big candy box.
Put the lid on the box.

★ ★ ★ ★ ★ ★ ★ ★ ★ ★ ★ ★ **Performance** ★ ★ ★ ★ ★ ★ ★ ★ ★ ★ ★ ★

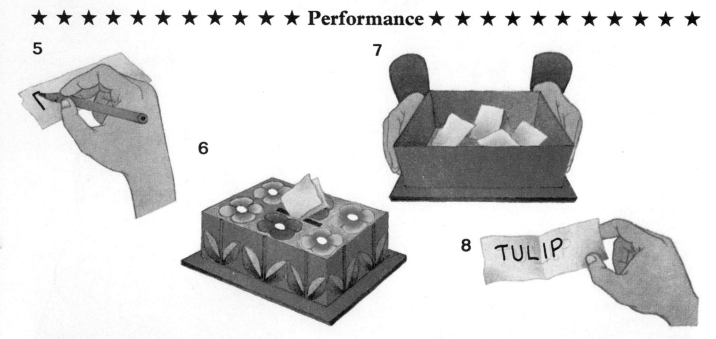

Tell everyone you can guess accurately.
Give out **pencils** and the blank slips of paper.

5. Ask your spectators to write the name of any flower on their slips of paper.

6. Then ask for the papers to be folded and put into the box through the slit in the lid.

Shake the box, and then remove the lid.

7. Ask someone to take out any slip.

8. You are able to tell the audience that the name of the flower on the slip is "tulip."
(Don't let anyone see the little box under the big lid – that's where the other slips are!)

Wash-off picture

This method of painting makes a picture seem to come from nowhere! Lightly draw a design in **pencil** on a sheet of **rough-textured white paper.**
Fix it to a **window** with **masking tape** and fill in the drawing with **white poster paint** and a **brush.**
Remove the picture from the window and let it dry.

Paint over the whole sheet with **waterproof black India ink.**
Let the ink dry completely.
Run **cold water** over the paper and rub the painting gently with your finger. As the ink washes off the parts you painted, an unusual picture will appear.

Snowball

Have snow all year around! To make the snowball, first **ask an adult** for a **white plastic bag.** Remember *never* put a plastic bag over your head and *never* let a baby play with one.

1. Use **scissors** to cut up part of the plastic bag into tiny snippets.
2. Put the snippets into a **screw-top jar** and fill it almost to the top with **water.**

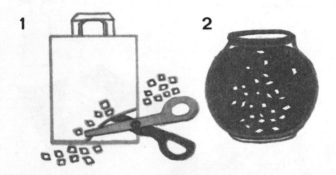

3. Use **household cement** to stick a **small plastic toy** to the underside of the lid. Let the cement dry. Screw the lid tightly to the jar and turn the snowball upside down to make the snow fall.

3

Nonstop twirler

Hang this snaky twirler in your bedroom and it will keep moving while you're fast asleep.
1. Use a **pencil** to draw around a **small plate** on **thin cardboard.**
2. Cut out the circle and make a small hole in the center with the point of the **scissors.**
Working outward from the middle, draw a spiral on the cardboard as shown.
3. Cut along the spiral from the edge of the cardboard to the center.
Tie a knot in one end of a piece of **string.**
4. Thread the string through the center hole.
Fix the other end of the string to the ceiling with **masking tape.** If you hang the twirler over a radiator the heat will make it turn. *Do not hang it over any other kind of heat or fire.*

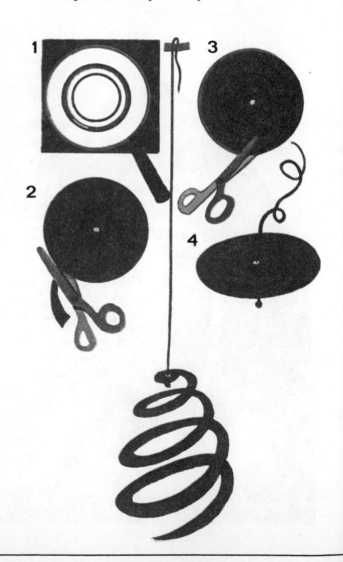

Paper doll chains

Chains of dolls make pretty decorations.

1. Fold a strip of **paper** into zigzag pleats as shown. Fold all the pleats together.

2. With a **pencil,** draw a doll on the top pleat. Let the arms go off the sides of the paper.

3. With **scissors,** cut around the shape through all the paper folds. Do not cut the ends of the arms.

Open out the paper.

4. Color the dolls with **crayons or colored pencils.**

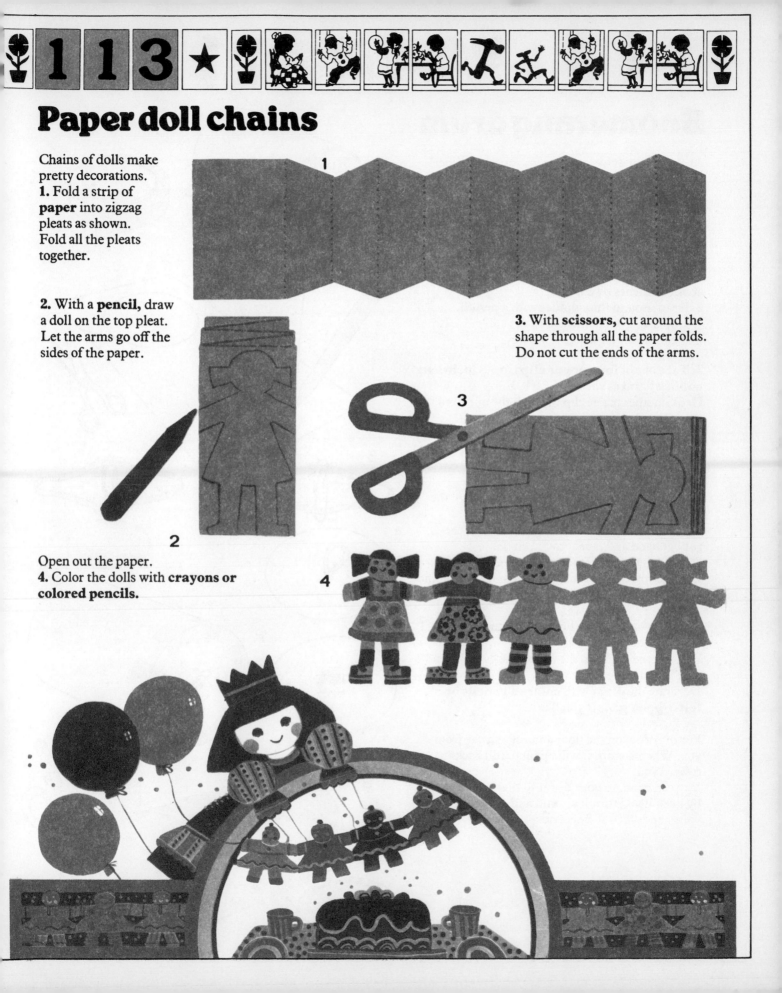

Boomerang drum

As this drum moves away from you, the rubber band inside it stores up the energy needed to drive it back again.

1. Roll up a strip of **stiff paper** 40 inches by 6 inches into a cylinder about 4 inches in diameter. Fix the seam with **cellophane tape.**
Stand the cylinder on a piece of **stiff cardboard** about 12 inches by 6 inches.
2. Draw around the cylinder with a **pencil.**
Use **scissors** to cut out the circle.
Cut another circle in the same way.

3. Tape one of **four paper clips** to a **3 inch-long rubber band** as shown.
Hook another paper clip through the one fixed to the rubber band.
4. Mold a lump of **plasticine** around the second clip. With the point of the scissors, make a small hole in the middle of each cardboard circle.

5. Push one end of the rubber band through the hole in one cardboard circle.
6. Thread a paper clip through the end of the rubber band and tape it to the circle.
7. Tape the circle to the end of the cylinder.
Pull the spare end of the rubber band through the cylinder.

8. Push it through the hole in the other circle and tape it to the cardboard.
Position the circle on the end of the cylinder and tape it into place.
Decorate the drum with **colored pencils or felt-tipped pens** if you like.

Put the drum on the floor and roll it away from you. When it stops it will begin to roll back toward you.
You can wind up your drum so that it rolls along by itself if you turn it around and around in your hands for a few seconds.

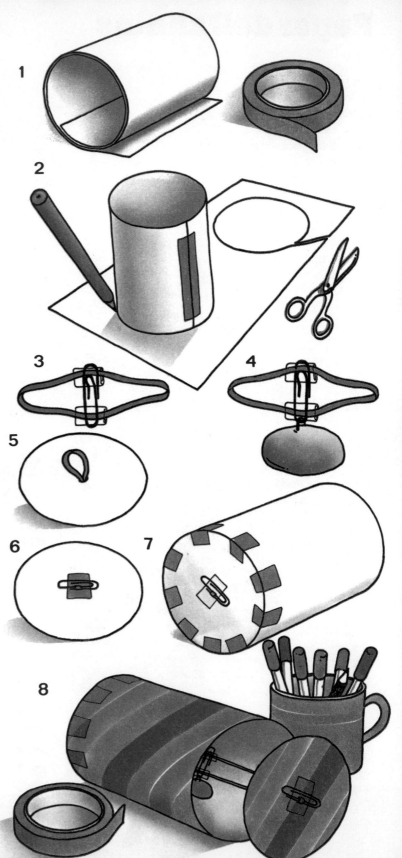

Sugar wall

Try a little experiment to see how waterproofing functions in the brickwork of a house.
Ask an adult if you can have some **sugar cubes** and some **cold coffee or tea.**
Build a wall of sugar cubes in a **shallow dish.**
Cut a piece of **plastic** big enough to cover the top row of the wall.
Build another wall of sugar cubes in the dish, putting the piece of plastic between the first and second rows of sugar cubes.
Pour a little cold coffee or tea into the dish.
The first wall you built will soak up the liquid and turn completely brown.
The second wall will be protected above its layer of waterproof plastic and only the bottom row will soak up the liquid.

Floating egg

Ask your friends if they can make an egg float in water.
Usually, when anyone puts an egg in water it sinks.
Now show them how to make it float.
Add **salt** to a **glass of water** and stir it with a **spoon** until no more salt will dissolve.
Gently put the **egg** in the salty water and it will float!

The egg floats because salty water is heavier than tap water.
A heavy liquid supports more weight than a light one.
For the same reason, a swimmer floats more easily in the salty sea than in fresh water.

Spot the ring

Here is a party game that can be played by very young children as well as older ones.

You will need **several yards of string** and a **curtain ring.** Slide the ring on the string; tie the ends together, making a huge loop.

Everyone sits in a circle except one player who stands in the middle. He or she is the guesser. When the guesser says "Go!" the other players run the string through their hands so that the ring moves around the circle.

When the guesser calls "Stop!" everyone closes their hands over the string. The guesser then has two guesses to find out who has the ring.

If the guesser is right the player holding the ring goes into the middle. If the guesser is wrong he or she is out and sits down in the middle.

The other players then choose another guesser.

Pea race

This is a game for an even number of players. You will need as many **saucers** and **drinking straws** as there are players, and a package of **dried peas. Get an adult** to check that all the peas you use for the game are *larger than the openings of the straws.* Otherwise, you might accidentally suck a pea into your throat. Here is how four people play:

Put two saucers with ten peas in each of them on one side of the room. Two players stand beside these saucers.

Each player has a partner who stands near an empty saucer on the opposite side of the room. All the players have a drinking straw. The first players have to get their ten peas into their partners' saucers by sucking one pea at a time onto the end of the straws and carrying it across the room.

The partners have to bring all ten peas back. The first pair to finish wins the game.

Batter-up game

This is a game for a sunny day. Mark a small circle on the ground with **chalk or a stick.**
A batter, holding a **piece of wood,** stands inside the circle.
The other players form a ring about 2½ yards away from the batter.
One of the players has a **rubber ball or tennis ball.**
The ball must be rolled along the ground or bounced at the batter, who has to try and strike it away with the bat.
The batter must not move his or her feet at all.
The ball can be passed back and forth among the other players. They must try to hit the batter's legs below the knees with it.
The batter needs to be very alert in this game. The ball can be thrown at the back of the legs where it is difficult to fend off. By hitting the ball a long way the batter can gain some breathing time. If someone hits the batter or makes him or her lose balance, then that player takes a turn with the bat.

Fine and feathery

Birds' feathers are incredibly varied and once you have looked at a few you will begin to see how lovely they are. When you are in the country or by the seashore watch out for the feathers of wild birds. Look in library books about birds to identify the feathers you find. Or visit a local butcher shop and ask for duck, goose, chicken or turkey feathers for your collection. If you have just a few feathers, why not make a feather duster for helping with the dusting?

Feather duster
Simply use **cellophane tape** to bind the **feathers** to a **bamboo or cane rod** about 1 foot long.

Feather choker
Show off your most beautiful feathers by combining them with ribbon and **beads.**

Slip a bead on each end of some **short pieces of ribbon or cord.** Knot the ends.

1. Using a **needle** and **thread,** sew one feather to the middle of each length of ribbon or cord.

2. Tie the ribbon or cord into a bow. Slip a bead on each end of a piece of **wide ribbon** about 15 inches long and knot the ends.

3. Sew each feathery bow to the ribbon. Wear your choker to a special party.

More mail please!

Stamp collecting is a popular hobby everywhere. Some stamps are collected because they are rare and valuable and others are saved up because of their attractive designs.

You could choose a subject, or a theme, for your own collection – what about stamps showing animals, or sports or famous paintings?

The best way to look at the designs on stamps is through a magnifying glass.

Removing stamps

Never tear **stamps** from an envelope.

1. Use **scissors** to cut the stamp off, leaving ¾ inch of paper all around.

Fill a **shallow dish** with **cold water.**

2. Float your stamps in it, face upward, for about 15 minutes. Lift out the stamps with **tweezers.**

Peel off the paper. Put the stamps, face downward, on a sheet of **blotting paper.** Let them dry.

3. Press them between the pages of an **old book** overnight.

Zigzag folder

Most people put their stamps in an album. A folder is an interesting and different idea.

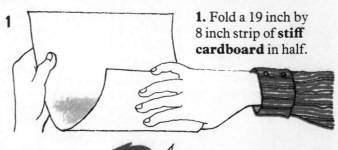

1. Fold a 19 inch by 8 inch strip of **stiff cardboard** in half.

2. Fold one half backward in half again.

3. Fold the other half neatly backward in the same way. Stand the cardboard up in a zigzag.

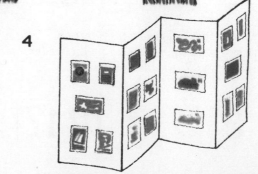

4. Stick your stamps to **stamp hinges** and fix them to the folder.

Odd one out

Think where you would find all these things, and then decide which is the odd one out in the group.
(The answer is given in the back of the book.)

Missing number

Which number should go in the blank square?

| 1 | 2 | 3 | 4 | ? | 6 |

Five, because each number increases by one.
The puzzle below is similar, but a tiny bit harder.
Which number goes in the blank square?

| 2 | 3 | 5 | ? | 12 | 17 |

(The answer is in the back of the book.)

Puzzling trio

Find **one colored and two white scarves or handkerchiefs.** Knot them together so that two white ones are together and the colored one is at the end.
Can you put the colored scarf between the two white ones without untieing any knots?
Here's a clue: one of the Magic projects in the previous pages showed a way of tieing ribbons to perform a similar trick.
(The method is given in the back of the book.)

Tied in knots

To work this puzzle out, test it.
You will need a friend to help you
and two pieces of **string,** each
about 32 inches long.
Use one length of string to tie your
friend's wrists together loosely.
Loop the second length of string
over the first length, and then
loosely tie your own wrists together
with the second length.
Can you and your friend work out
how to untangle yourselves without
breaking or untieing the string?
(The Answers in the back of the
book show how it's done.)

Six buckets

Here is a row of six buckets. The first three
buckets have water in them but the last three
are empty.
By touching only one bucket, how can you make
the row have alternate full and empty buckets?
(There is a very simple solution and it is given in
the back of the book.)

Snatch a match

Arrange **12 used matches** to make four equal
squares as shown.
By moving only *three* matches, try to make three
equal squares.
(The way to do it is shown in the back of the book.)

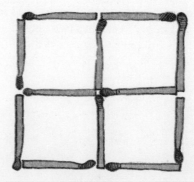

Jumping coin

Make a coin move without touching it.
Put a **small coin** on top of a **bottle** that has some **soda or other bubbly drink** in it.
Hold the bottle tightly in both hands around the part that contains the drink.
The coin will begin to jump up and down.
The warmth of your hands makes the gas in the drink expand. As it tries to escape from the bottle, it pushes up the coin.

Mighty balloon

This specially-prepared balloon won't burst when you push a **pin** in at the right place.
Put a square of **transparent cellophane tape** on an **inflated balloon.**

★ ★ ★ ★ Performance ★ ★ ★ ★

Tell your audience that you have an unburstable balloon. (They probably won't believe you.)
Push a pin into the balloon through the tape.
The balloon won't burst.

Salt and pepper

No secret preparation is needed for this trick.
Use a **pencil** to write "Salt," "Pepper," "Salt" on a piece of **thin cardboard.** Tear the cardboard in three and put the pieces in a **box.**
Tell your audience you can read the words without looking, then close your eyes and pick the card which says "Pepper."
Picking the right card is easy. Because it is in the middle, the "Pepper" card has two jagged edges when torn. All you have to do is feel the edges of the cards in the box.

Stick-up

This pencil seems to stick to your hand.
Show the spectators a **pencil** in your left hand, turning the back of your hand toward them.
Grasp your left wrist with your right hand.
The audience now sees the pencil stuck to it.

What no one sees is your right forefinger holding the pencil in your left palm.

Butterfly net

With this simple net you can catch butterflies, make drawings and identify them from library books. *Never kill butterflies.*

1. With **scissors,** cut the fine mesh from an **old plastic sieve** so that only the frame and handle are left.

1

2. With **string,** bind the handle to a **bamboo or cane rod** 20 inches long.

2

3. Use a **tape measure** to measure the frame's circumference.

3

4. Cut a piece of **fine mesh net** into a triangle. The top of the net should be the same measurement as the circumference of the frame.

4

10 ins

5

Use a **needle** and **thread** to join the sides of the net.
5. Attach it to the frame by sewing over the frame and through the top of the net.

Butterfly farm

Caterpillars, as everyone knows, change into butterflies. If you prepare a special cage and find a caterpillar in the summer, you can watch this change yourself.

1. Ask an adult to punch some holes in the lid of a **shallow tin** with an **awl or a hammer and nail.** With **string** and a **ruler,** measure the tin's circumference.

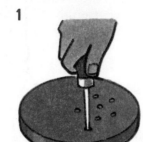

2. Cut a piece of **clear, stiff plastic or acetate** (from an art supply store) 20 inches high and 1 inch wider than the tin's circumference.

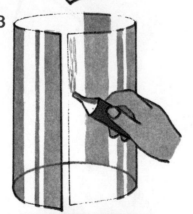

3. Use **household cement** to join the edges of the plastic, overlapping them so that the plastic cylinder will just fit into the base of the tin. Put the cylinder in the base of the tin. Cut a **nylon stocking** to fit over the top.

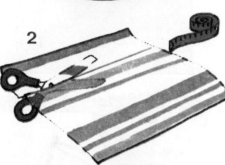

4. Carefully put the lid of the tin on the cylinder.

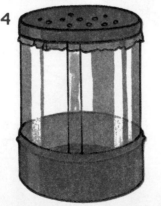

5. Put a layer of **soil** in the tin.

6. Put a **small jar of water** into the soil. Your cage is ready. Now look on grasses and plants or in hedges for a **caterpillar.** (A clue is chewed leaves.) Take some of the plant, too. This is the **caterpillar's food.**

7. Put the plant in the jar of water to keep it fresh and put your caterpillar on the plant. Put in fresh food when the caterpillar has eaten the leaves. When the butterfly emerges, set it free.

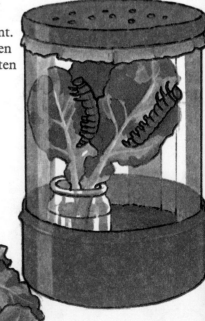

Pressed flowers

If you choose perfect flowers for pressing, you can make all kinds of beautiful things.

Here's how to press flowers and how to make a calendar. Other ways of using pressed flowers are shown in Projects 186 and 308.

1. Separate **flowers** from their stems.

Lay them face down between **sheets of newspaper.**

2. Put **books** on top and leave the flowers for a few days. Change the newspaper and leave them for another few days.

Calender

Use **glue** to stick a **calendar** on the bottom half of a sheet of **colored cardboard.**

1. Draw a design on the top in **pencil.**

2. Carefully glue some **pressed flowers** on your design.

Bouncing nuts

A well-known game (see Project 323) is played with horse chestnuts. You can also make a bouncing mobile with them.

Collect some **horse chestnuts** in the autumn and varnish them with **polyurethane varnish** and a **brush** to help preserve their color. **Ask an adult** to pierce a hole through each nut with a **meat skewer.**

You will need a few pieces of **thin elastic.** Knot one end of each. Thread a few nuts onto each elastic, tieing a knot before and after each nut. Tie the lengths of elastic around a **bamboo or cane rod.** Use **string** to suspend the rod from a curtain rod and watch the chestnuts bounce.

All eyes

Grow a potato into an attractive trailing plant.

Choose a **potato with lots of "eyes."**

Push **toothpicks** into the potato and rest it in a **jar of water** so that the bottom of the potato just touches the water.

Put the jar in a cool, dark place until the potato has sprouted both roots and shoots.

When it is ready, use a **knife** to cut off all but one or two of the potato shoots.

Put some **pebbles** in the bottom of a **flowerpot.** Fill the pot with **damp potting soil.**

Then plant the potato in the pot. Don't forget to water it when the soil feels dry.

Spatter pictures

This can be messy, so be sure to wear an **apron** and remember to clean up afterwards.

1. Spread out a sheet of **newspaper** and lay a sheet of **white or colored paper** on it.

2. Use **pins** to fix a **leaf or another flat object** to the paper.

Mix some **poster paint** with a little **water**. Don't make it too thin.

Dip an **old toothbrush** in the paint. Hold an **old comb** over the paper and rub the toothbrush gently back and forth across the teeth of the comb.

1

2

When the paper is spattered all over, wait three minutes and then lift off the leaf.

3. Pin a **second leaf or another flat object** to the paper, overlapping the first shape a little. Spatter it with a different color.

If you use several colors, spatter each one *lightly* or your picture will soon get messy.

3

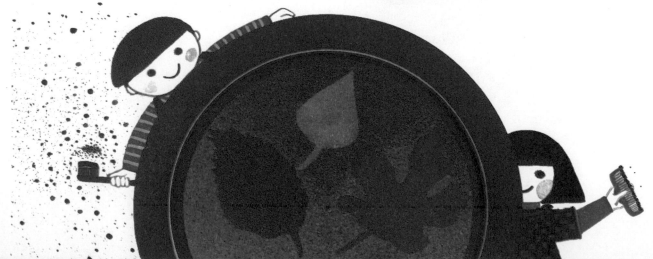

Cook a frame

This picture frame is only for looking at, not for eating! **Ask an adult** to help you cook it.

1. Use a **rolling pin** to roll out the **dough** until it is ½ inch thick.

Trim it to a square with a **kitchen knife** and keep the left-over scraps.

1

Center a **picture** on the square.

2. With the knife, mark an outline a bit larger than the picture all around.

3

3. Press with your fingertips inside the outline to make a slight hollow.

Dough recipe

1 cup hot water
¾ cup salt
3 cups flour

Mix the salt and water in a **bowl.** Let it cool. Mix in the flour with your hands. Work fast – this dough soon gets brittle!

---

4. Roll and cut the dough scraps into little balls, thin sausages and other shapes.

Dab the back of the shapes with a little **water** and press them onto the dough frame.

4

Cook the frame until it is quite dry (30–40 minutes) in an **oven** set at 375°.

5. Paint the frame with **acrylic paints** and use **glue** to stick the picture in the hollow.

5

Water cooler

See how to keep water cool in the sunshine.
You will need **two glass jars** and **two cotton dish towels**.
1. Fill both glass jars with **water**.

Wrap a towel around one glass jar.
2. Soak the other towel in water and wrap it tightly around the other glass jar.
Put both jars outside in the sun. (Or put them in a warm place.)

Feel the wet dish towel about every half hour.
3. When it is dry, take off both towels and feel the jars with your hands.
The jar that was wrapped in the wet towel will feel cooler than the other jar.

This is because the water in the wet dish towel *evaporates* (or mixes with the dry air around the towel). As it does this, it draws heat from the jar inside, so keeping the jar cool.
A similar thing happens when you perspire: as the sweat evaporates from your skin, it draws heat from your body and cools you down.

Soft potato

Ask a friend to try to push an ordinary **drinking straw** into a **raw potato.**
The straw will probably bend and the potato will remain exactly the same.
Now you can show how it's done.
Grip the straw firmly between your thumb and first finger about an inch from one end.
Quickly thrust the straw at the potato.
You should make a hole in the potato.
Your friend will be amazed, so explain why the straw pierces the potato.
When you grip and thrust quickly in this way, air is held inside the straw. This makes the sides of the straw stronger, which prevents it from bending as it hits the potato.

Draw an oval

Draw an oval using a **compass.**
Roll a piece of **stiff cardboard** about 12 inches by 8 inches into a cylinder.
Put **masking tape** on the seam.
Roll a sheet of **paper** the same size around the cylinder and fix the seam with masking tape.
Set a compass
to a radius of about
3 inches.
Push the point of the
compass into the
paper and cardboard.
Turn the **pencil** around.
Remove the compass
and unwrap the paper.
You have an oval!

Spinning vision

This game is a lot of fun and shows you how your brain looks at pictures or images.
Use a **pencil** and a **compass** to draw a circle 6 inches across on **stiff cardboard.**
1. Cut it out with **scissors.** Cut the scraps into several ¾ inch squares.
Cut a **paper** circle 5½ inches in diameter.

2. Fold the paper circle in half.
Repeat this step four more times.
Open out the paper circle and lay it on the cardboard circle.

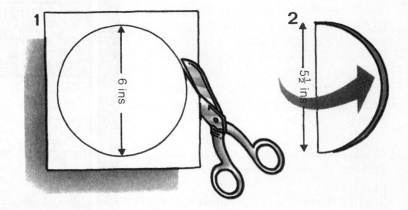

1

6 ins

2

5½ ins

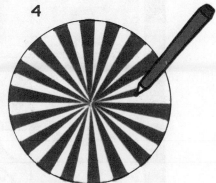

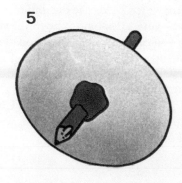

3

4

5

3. Use a **felt-tipped pen** to mark equal sections on the cardboard, using the paper folds as a guide. Join the marks across the circle.

4. Color the alternate sections. Make a hole in the center of the cardboard circle with the point of the scissors.

Push a pencil through the hole.
5. Mold **plasticine** around the pencil and onto the cardboard about 1½ inches from the sharpened end.

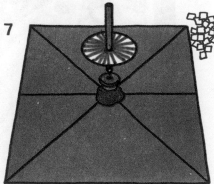

6

7

6. Divide a **big sheet of paper** (about 16 inches square) into eight equal segments as shown.

Fix **an empty spool** to the middle of the paper with plasticine.
7. Stand the pencil in it.

How to play
Spin the circle quickly.
Drop a **square of cardboard** on it.
It will fly off onto the board.
See if you can hit each segment.

When you spin the circle the white and colored segments seem to mix together. That's because each time a picture reaches your brain it stays there for a fraction of a second. This is called *persistence of vision*.

Forgotten planet

Your spaceship has crash-landed on a strange planet that is still covered with the people and monsters from prehistoric times.

You need to reach Mission Control Headquarters to radio for help, but first you encounter a number of hazards on the way.

All the players take turns to throw a **die** and the first one to throw a six starts. Different-colored **counters** are used by the players.

Starting at square one, move your counter according to the number you have thrown on the die. Every time you land on a square which holds the bottom of a rocket, you can zoom to the top. Every time you meet the head of a monster, you must slide right down to the tip of its tail. You will also meet other helps and hazards on your journey.

The player who reaches Mission Control Headquarters (Square 100) first, wins the Forgotten Planet game.

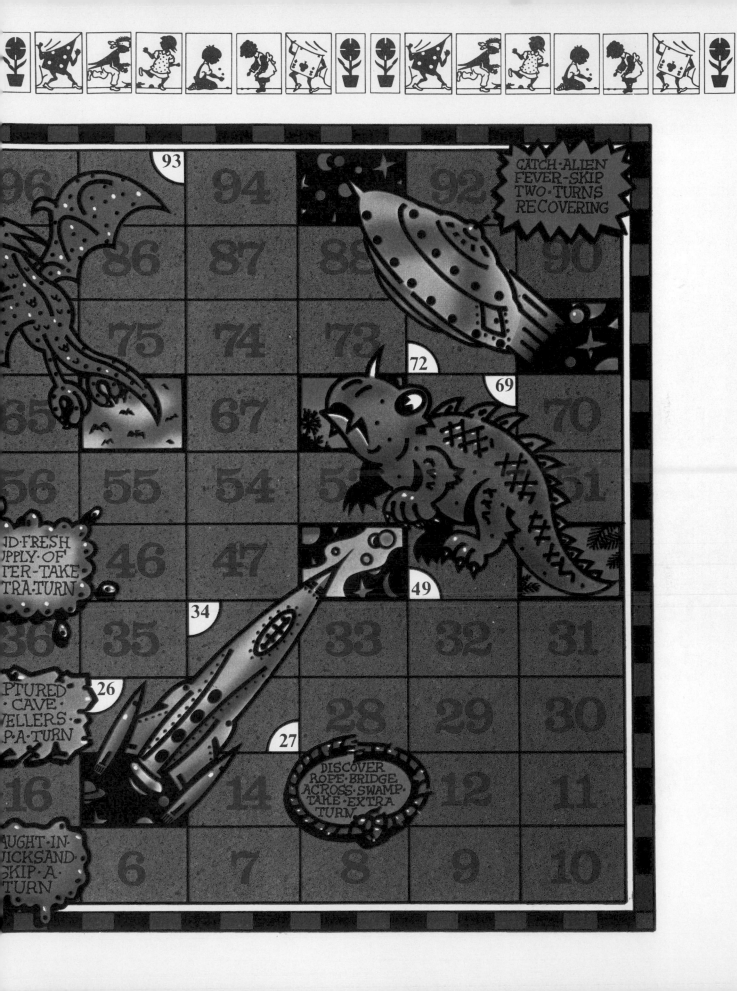

Sliding coins

Arrange **six coins** in a pyramid as shown.
By *sliding* only four coins to different places, make
the pyramid into a circle.

Rule: when moving a coin into a new position,
it *must* touch two other coins.
(The method is shown in the back of the book.)

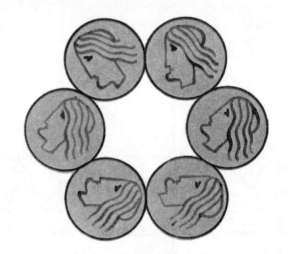

Take your pick

Can you name the fruits on this strange tree?
(The fruits are given in the Answers in the back of
the book.)

Eskimo family

Here is a puzzle set in Alaska where the Eskimo
people live in ice houses called *igloos*.
A little Eskimo and a big Eskimo are building a
new igloo together.
They cut the blocks of ice to size, and then
arrange them one on top of the other.
The little Eskimo is the big Eskimo's son.
But the big Eskimo is not the little Eskimo's
father.
Who is the big Eskimo? (That is, can you tell
what is the family relationship between the big
and the little Eskimo?)
(The answer is given in the back of the book.)

Hat trick

Each one of these characters is wearing the wrong hat. Can you dress them correctly?
(The answers are given in the back of the book.)

sailor

American Indian

cowpuncher

Oriental

clown

football player

Birthday cake

How can you cut this cake into eight equal portions by making only three cuts?
A clue: four pieces would have no icing.
(The solution is given in the Answers at the back of the book.)

A dotty one

Can you join all the dots by drawing only four straight lines? You must not take your **pencil** off the **paper** but you can draw beyond the frame of the dots if you want to.
(Look in the back of the book for the method.)

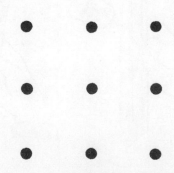

Family photographs

Collecting photographs can be an amusing hobby. Very old portrait photographs might make you laugh because the people look so stiff. They had to sit absolutely still for quite a few minutes while a photograph was taken.

You could make a collection of family photographs starting from recently-taken ones and going back to the oldest ones you can find. Ask your parents, grandparents or aunts and uncles for photographs. Look at the photographs closely to see how fashions and hairstyles have changed or how home furnishings or street scenes are different today. Don't forget to look for family resemblances – who do you think you look like in your family?

Frames
Most people keep their photographs in an album but you might like to make frames for the most interesting photographs in your collection.

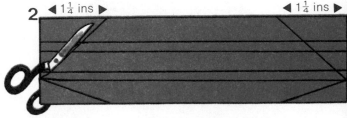

Use **scissors** to cut two sheets of **paper** 7 inches by $1\frac{5}{8}$ inches and two sheets $6\frac{1}{4}$ inches by $1\frac{5}{8}$ inches.

1. With a **ruler** and **pencil,** mark four lines across each sheet of paper at intervals of $\frac{3}{8}$, $\frac{1}{4}$, $\frac{3}{8}$, $\frac{1}{4}$ and $\frac{3}{8}$ inches as shown.

Mark $1\frac{1}{4}$ inches across the top and bottom corners of the sheets.
2. Cut off these corners as shown.

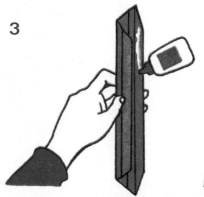

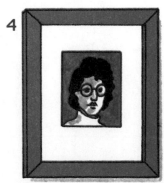

3. Fold each sheet along the lines, overlap the two long edges and use **glue** to stick them together.

Cut a sheet of **white cardboard** $6\frac{3}{4}$ inches by 6 inches.
4. Glue the folded paper frame around the cardboard, then glue your **photograph** in the middle.

Seed jewelry

There are plenty of places to look for seeds if you want to collect them as a hobby. Look in the countryside, the garden or park after plants have flowered. In the autumn you can find seeds that have fallen from trees such as beech and oak. Or save the pits and seeds from fruit you have eaten. Once you have collected a variety of seeds, why not make some jewelry with them? Tiny melon, orange or apple seeds are pretty enough for a necklace or brooch.
Always wash and dry pits or seeds first.

Seed necklace
Thread a **needle** with a piece of **thin elastic** and tie a knot in one end.
Push the needle into **melon or apple seeds** and thread them onto the elastic.
When you have enough, remove the needle and tie the ends. of the elastic together.

Seed brooch
Cut a piece of **stiff cardboard** to the shape you want.
1. Fix a **safety pin** to the back of it with **masking tape.**

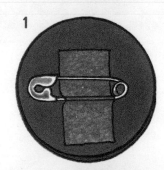

2. Arrange **small seeds** (apple, orange or melon) on the front.
Use **glue** to stick each one into place.
Let the glue dry.
(See Project 211 for some more ideas.)

Quick decals

Decals are a form of advertising. If you ask nicely and explain that you are collecting decals, most firms will give you a few. Ask at travel agents, garages and stores. Or you might be able to buy some at candy stores and dime stores.
Use them to decorate books, belts or an apron.

Decal apron
Here's an idea for a very unusual apron. Make it for yourself or as a gift for someone else.

Use **scissors** to cut out the shape of the apron from **oil cloth or plastic-coated cloth.**
(You don't need to hem this kind.)
Cut two long pieces of **twill tape** to make apron ties and one short piece to go around the neck.
With a **needle** and **strong thread,** sew the pieces of tape to the apron.
Now decorate the apron with **decals.** You'll find that they stick very easily to plastic.

Silhouette portrait

A *silhouette* is an outline. Here is an easy way to make a silhouette portrait of your friend.

1. Ask a friend to sit sideways against a **wall.**

2. Fix a sheet of **paper** to the wall with **masking tape.**

3. Take the lampshade off a **table lamp.**

4. Make the room as dark as possible by closing doors and drawing curtains.

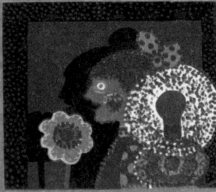

5. Switch on the lamp and move it close to your friend.

6. Outline the shadow with **pencil.** Cut it out with **scissors** and use **glue** to stick it to **cardboard.**

Glue a frame of **colored paper** around the picture.

Scratch painting

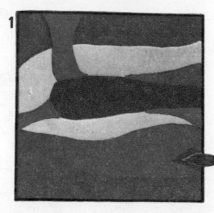

This is an amazing kind of painting because the colors actually appear from behind a thick surface of black wax crayon.

1. Using **poster or acrylic paints,** make big blocks of color on a sheet of **thick paper.** Completely cover the paper with paint.

2. When the paint is quite dry, scribble all over the paper with **black wax crayon.** Press down hard and completely cover the painted colors with crayon.

With a **nail or a metal knitting needle** (or any other sharp object) scratch a picture in the wax so that the colors appear.

Pond study

If you are lucky enough to have a pond in your garden or near your home, you can discover the fascinating world that exists beneath the water.

Make a net by binding a **wire sieve** to a 1 yard-long **pole** with **strong string.** Or you can make a butterfly net as shown in Project 132. You will also need a **magnifying glass,** a **white dish** for viewing specimens and a **jar** for taking specimens home with you.
Ask an adult to come with you if the pond is deep, and approach it carefully. First watch the surface of the pond. You should be able to see tiny insects moving on the water. You may see the *larvae* (grubs) of other insects hanging below the surface of the water.
Now take your net and scoop it into the water around the edge of the pond. Then stretch out and scoop into the middle of the pond. (Be careful you don't lose your balance!) You might catch newts, tadpoles and beetles as well as tinier plants and animals in this way.

1. Put anything you catch into the dish and examine it with the magnifying glass. Then you could put the creature back in the pond.

2. If you want to take a few newts or tadpoles home, prepare a jar for them. Put some **sand** in the bottom of the jar, plant some **pondweed** in it and fill the jar with **water.** Feed the newts, with worms.
Tadpoles eat meat which you can hang from the edge of the jar with string.

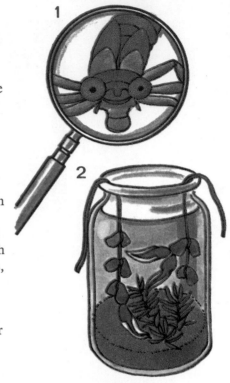

Dial-a-sun

Before clocks and watches were invented, everyone measured time by the sun. Make a sundial and do the same.

Press a lump of **plasticine** onto the middle of a sheet of **cardboard** about 1 foot square.
1. Push the blunt end of a **pencil** into the plasticine at an angle.

Put the sundial outside in the sun.
Use a **clock or watch** to tell the time.
2. On the hour, make a mark at the point where the shadow of the pencil falls on the cardboard.

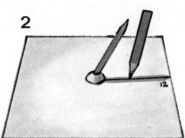

3. At every half-hour after that, write the time where the shadow falls.
Do this from early morning till sunset.

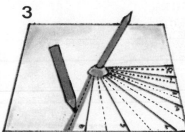

4. Once you have marked your sundial, you can tell the time without a watch as long as the sun is shining. Always leave the sundial facing the same way. If you like, decorate the clock face and varnish the whole sundial.

Sweeping start

This is the sort of broom that witches were supposed to have flown on. You can use it to sweep up leaves, even if you can't fly!

Find a good **straight branch** about 1½ yards long.
1. Strip off any side branches.

2. Bind some **strong string** to the branch about 8 inches from one end.

Now tie the first layer of **long, sweepy twigs** to the branch, binding them tightly with more string.
Keep adding layers of twigs until your broom is thick.

3. Bind the outside layer very tightly, using lots of string.
You need to make a band of string at least 2 or 2½ inches wide.

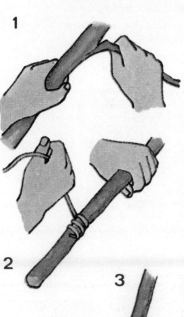

Flick book

This book changes from an empty book to a full stamp album and back again before your eyes! With **scissors** cut a narrow strip from the edge of every other page in a **blank notebook**.
1. On every double page where the short page falls on the right-hand side, stick some **stamps.**

1

2. Where the short page falls on the left, leave the pages completely blank.

2

★ ★ ★ Performance ★ ★ ★

3. Hold the book in front of you and flick through the pages with your left hand. The book appears to be full of stamps.
4. Turn the book over and flick the pages the other way, with your right hand. The book now appears to be empty.

3   **4**

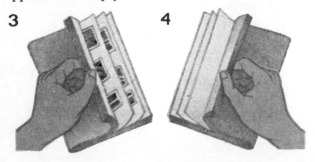

Mathemagic

Your audience will have to do some work, too, when you perform this trick.

★ ★ ★ Performance ★ ★ ★

1

Hand a friend a sheet of **paper** and a **pencil**.
1. Ask your friend to draw a square and write in it any number from one to nine, without letting you see it.

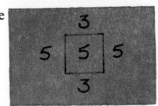

2. Tell your friend to write the same number to the right and the left of the square.

2

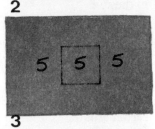

3. Now ask him to write the figure 3 above and below the square.

3

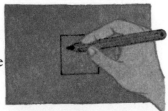

Now your friend should add up all the numbers on the sheet of paper and tell you the total.
As soon as you know the total, you can tell your friend the number he or she originally wrote in the square.

How you do it
Divide your friend's total by three.
Take away two and the answer is the number in the square.
In the example shown in the pictures, your friend will tell you that the total is 21 (5+5+5+3+3). When you divide by three you get seven (21÷3); then seven minus two equals five (7—2=5).

All change

Find the two, three, four and five of hearts and of spades in an **old deck of cards**.
1. Use **scissors** to cut the two, three and four of hearts in half from corner to corner.

1

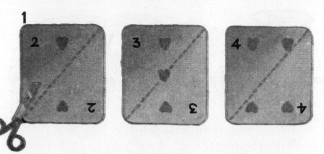

2. Use **glue** to stick one half of each card to the face of the two, three and four of spades.

2

3. Arrange the three special cards in a fan shape. Place a five of hearts on top so it looks as if you are holding the two, three, four and five of hearts. Hide the five of spades at the back of the fan.

3

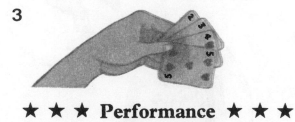

★ ★ ★ Performance ★ ★ ★

Show the red cards to your audience, then close the cards into a small pack.
Turn the cards over.
Put the five of hearts to the back of the pack.
Bring the five of spades to the front.
Turn the pack upside down.
Open out the cards, making sure you keep the five of hearts hidden. It will look as if they have changed from red to black.

Ring vanish

Keep this trick up your sleeve for moments when you and your friends are feeling bored!
Tie a piece of **elastic** to a **ring**. The elastic should be about three-quarters the length of your arm.
1. Tie the other end of the elastic to a **safety pin**.

1

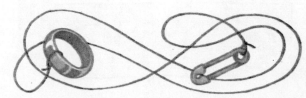

Fasten the pin inside the top of the right sleeve of your sweater.
2. Put the ring on one of your right fingers and then put on your sweater.

2

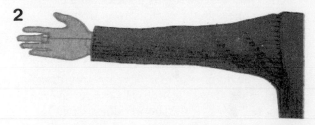

★ ★ ★ Performance ★ ★ ★

3. Take the ring off your finger with the left hand. Be careful not to show the elastic.
Hold the ring between your right forefinger and thumb. Pretend to throw the ring into the air. As you let go it disappears (up your sleeve)!

3

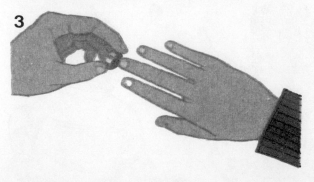

Marble bridges

Here is a new way of playing marbles, but you need to make a bridge before you start playing. To make the bridge, find an old **shoe box.** With a **pencil,** draw four arches along one side. Then cut out the arches with **scissors,** and write a number above each one.

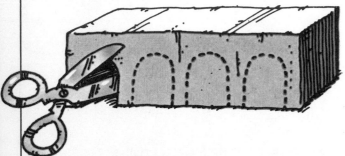

To play the game, each player should have an equal number of **marbles.** One player is the "bridge keeper" but he does not shoot. With a **piece of string or a ruler,** make a starting line about two yards away from the bridge. Each player in turn tries to shoot a marble into one of the arches. For each marble that goes through, he receives from the bridge keeper the number of marbles corresponding to the number above the arch. He also receives his "shooter" back. If the shooter does not go through the arch, it belongs to the bridge keeper. The game ends when each player has had ten shots The player with the most marbles is the winner.

What's missing?

Any number of people can play this game, but they all need a sharp eye and good memory. Find twenty or more **small household objects** – laundry powder, food cans, soap bars and so on –

but don't forget to **ask an adult** before you raid the cabinets. Put all the objects on a table. Give every player a piece of **paper** and a **pencil.** Pick someone to be an observer. The players have a good look at the objects on the table. Then they all leave the room except one player and the observer. The player who is left removes one object from the table. The observer writes down the name of the object and puts it out of sight. The other players return and write down what is missing from the table. All the players take turns removing an object. Then they compare their lists with the observer's list. The one with the most correct missing objects is the winner.

Twenty questions

Thinking hard can be fun. Choose your questions carefully to win this game.
One player thinks of an object, but must not say what it is. The only thing that player tells the others is whether it is animal, vegetable or mineral. For example, a whale and a fly are both animal. An onion is vegetable but so is a book because paper is made from trees. A can of baked beans is vegetable (beans) and mineral (can).
The other players can now ask twenty questions to try to find out what the object is. Questions must be phrased so that they can be answered with a "Yes" or a "No."
If the other players guess the object before twenty questions are up, someone else thinks of an object and the game starts again.

Hunt the beast

This is a good game for a party or for two friends. Two players are chosen as the "hunter" and "beast." Tie a **blindfold** around the hunter's eyes. The hunter holds a **rolled-up newspaper.** The hunter calls out "Where are you beast?" and the other player must roar like a wild animal and try to escape.
The hunter has to guess where the beast is and tries to whack him or her with the newspaper.
If the hunter succeeds in catching the beast, the players change places.
This game is best played out-of-doors, but if there are a lot of people indoors, they can form a circle to prevent people from bumping into the furniture.

Donkey's tail

This is a hilarious game for a party.
Find or draw a **large picture of a donkey** (or any other animal with a tail). Cut off the tail and stick a **push pin** through the top of it.
Then fix the picture to the wall with **thumbtacks or masking tape** at about eye level.
Make a blindfold with an **old scarf.** Each player in turn should be blindfolded and the tail put in his or her hand. Each must try to pin the tail as nearly as possible to the right place on the donkey. The other players can join in the game by giving directions, for example – "Move to the right," "Further down," or "You're getting warmer!" To make the game harder, the blindfolded player can be spun around a couple of times.

Potato people

You can make a potato family or even a royal potato family with some scraps from around the house. Collect together a **large, medium** and a **small potato.**

Using **pins** and **glue**, attach **buttons** for eyes, scraps of **cloth** for clothes and **yarn** for hair.
With **sequins, gold braid** and scraps of **velvet,** make the King and his Royal Potato Family.

Sound sense

The shape of this cone concentrates sound. You can use it as a megaphone to talk to people who are far away, or use it as an amplifier to listen to very quiet sounds.

1. Bend a **large piece of cardboard** about 20 inches by 16 inches to make a cone shape. Fix it with **cellophane tape.**

1

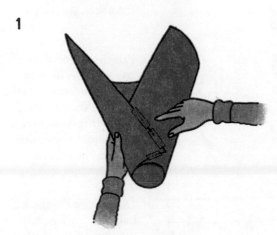

2. Bend a **smaller piece of cardboard** about 16 inches by 10 inches around to cover the gap in the cone. Stick it in place on the cone. Cut the corners with **scissors** to make the two ends of the cone into neat circles.

2

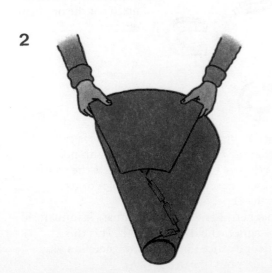

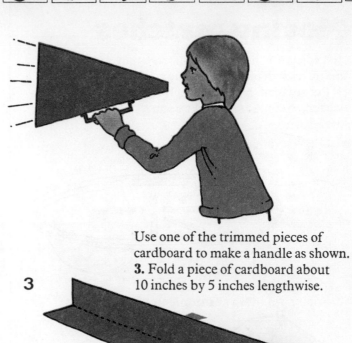

Use one of the trimmed pieces of cardboard to make a handle as shown.

3. Fold a piece of cardboard about 10 inches by 5 inches lengthwise.

3

4

4. Make four cuts on both sides of the cardboard strip about 2 inches from each end.

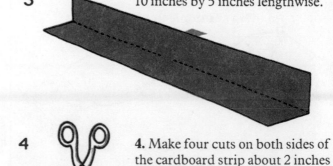

5

5. Fold back the flaps you have made and tuck them underneath. Fix them strongly with cellophane tape.

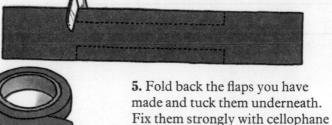

6

6. Bend the handle as shown and join it to the cone.

Moving matches

In Project 1 you can make matches move for a magic trick. Now find out why it happens.
1. Put **several matches** in a **bowl** almost full of **water,** to make a shape like a star.

2. Stick a **pin** into a **small piece of soap.**

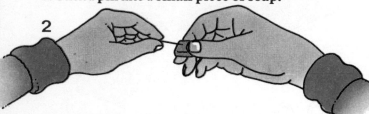

3. Gently dip the soap into the water at the center of the star of matches, taking care not to disturb them.
The matches will all move away from the soap.

The surface of the water pulls equally on all sides of the matches. This is called *surface tension.* When you dip the soap in the water a little of the soap dissolves. The surface tension of clean water is stronger than that of soapy water, so the matches are pulled outward by the clean water around them.

Flying magnets

Magnetize your friends with this experiment!

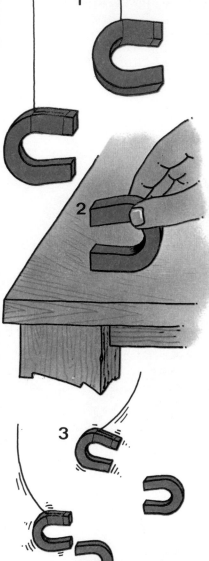

1. Fix one end of a length of **thread** to one end of a **magnet,** using **cellophane tape.** Fix the thread so that one end of the magnet hangs below the other.

Put the **second magnet** on its side on a table and hold it still.
2. Hold the first magnet by its thread so that it hangs just above the one on the table.

One of two things will happen: either the magnet on the thread will pull toward the magnet on the table, or it will move around trying to get away from it.
3. Turn the magnet on the table the other end up to get the opposite effect.

C-shaped magnets have two ends: one is called the north pole and the other is the south pole. The north pole of one magnet attracts the south pole of the other, but two north poles or two south poles repel one another.
(The magnetized needle in a compass is influenced by the magnetic field of the Earth. It is this magnetic influence that makes the needle swing around and point north.)

Clean air check

You can use this air pollution chart to check how clean the air is in your area.

1. Fold a **sheet of paper** lengthwise leaving it about ¾ inch wider on one side.

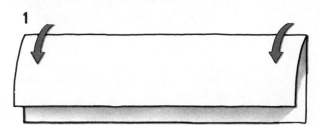

Measure the length of the paper with a **ruler.** Then divide the smaller section into seven equal sections, drawing lines where the divisions come.

2. Cut on the lines with **scissors.** Mark the days of the week on each section with a **felt-tipped pen.**

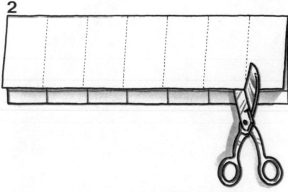

Put the chart by a window where you can leave it for a week without moving it.

3. Open up the flap for today. At the same time of day tomorrow, open up the second flap. Continue doing this for the next five days. At the end of the week, your chart will show the effects of an increasing number of days' exposure to air pollution.

Mon	Tues	Wed	Thur	Fri	Sat	Sun

Water heater

Discover how a greenhouse works by doing this simple experiment.

Fill **two yogurt containers** with **water.** Put them next to one another outside in the sun.

1. Put a **glass bowl or jar** upside down over one of the yogurt cups.

Leave the containers in the sunshine for about an hour. Then take the glass jar off the cup.

2. Feel the water in the two cups. The water in the container which was covered with glass will be warmer than the water in the other one.

The heat rays from the sun pass through the glass and heat up the water. The water then gives off heat but the rays are of a lower temperature than the sun's and cannot pass through the glass. So the space inside the glass heats up.

Salad sillies

You can have fun making these creatures and then eating them afterward.

Ask an adult before you begin searching in the vegetable bin. Pick out some **round vegetables and fruits** such as radishes and oranges to make heads and bodies. With a **kitchen knife,** cut up beans, carrots and celery to make arms, legs or wings. Join the pieces with **pins** or with **toothpicks.** Use toothpicks for antennae, legs and beaks.

Helpful Hints
Use hard fruits or vegetables for the body and legs of your creature so that it will be firm. Raisins pinned on make good eyes. Don't use vegetables that stain (like beets) unless you want to use the stain for effect. Try to pick fruits and vegetables that taste good together – but don't forget to take the pins out before you start eating! Make some more for your family.

Word consequences

Do you remember drawing consequences in Project 13 ? This time everyone helps write a funny story.
Tell everyone that the story will contain :
—two people
—what they were like
—where they met
—what they said to each other
—what happened – or the consequence.

Everyone needs a sheet of **paper** and a **pencil**. At the end of each of the following steps, each player folds over the paper so that nobody can see what was written and passes it on to the person sitting to the right.

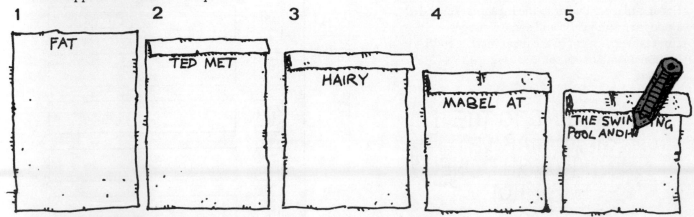

1 2 3 4 5

1. All the players start by writing at the top of their paper a word that describes what a person is like, such as "tired" or "fat."
2. Now write down the name of a male character, such as "Batman," "a rooster," or "Ken." Then write down the word "met."

3. Now write a word to describe the second person, such as "happy" or "hairy."
4. Now write the name of a female character. After this write down the word "at."
5. Now think of a meeting place – such as the "swimming pool" or the "police station." After writing this down, add "and he said to her."

6 7 8

6. Write down what he said to her – for example, "Do you come here often ?"
Then write down "and she said to him ."
7. Write down what she said – for example, "It's time for you to go."
Then add "and the consequence was."
8. Finally, write down the consequence of the meeting – such as "Their umbrellas blew away."

Now unfold the papers and read the stories out loud. They should make you laugh !

Shopping list

This game for two players may be easy to play but it is a hard test of memory.

First decide on the type of store you want for your game – a meat market, drugstore, or candy store, for example. Then take turns to build up a list of things you can buy at that type of store. The game proceeds this way:

First player: I went to the meat market and I bought a lamb chop.

Second player: I went to the meat market and I bought a lamb chop and some sausages.

First player: I went to the meat market and I bought a lamb chop, some sausages and a chicken.

Continue the game in this way with each player adding a new item to the list. At the same time each must remember all the other items on the list and get them in the right order.

The game goes on until someone is out. This happens when a player:
—cannot think of anything else to buy
—names something that cannot be bought in the type of store that has been chosen
—repeats something already on the list
—gets the order of items wrong
—forgets to name an item.

Airport anagrams

An *anagram* is a word whose letters have been scrambled so that you can't read it.

Some trouble makers have been at work in this airport. They have tried to make sure that nobody understands the names on the destinations board. Can you unscramble the names of the cities? (Check your answers in the back of the book.)

01 SIDAD ABAAB
02 WEN ROYK
03 DRIMAD
04 DYSENY
05 HIDEL
06 SPIRA

Pair the robots

A whole crowd of robots has just landed on Earth. To make it even more confusing for the
Earthlings, some robots are identical in everything except color.
Can you find the identical pairs ? (The answers are in the back of the book.)

Matchbox mix

Matchbox labels are as interesting to collect as stamps, and cover as many different subjects.

Start your collection by looking around your own house for empty matchboxes and asking your friends and relatives to save theirs for you.

If you know anyone who is going abroad, ask them to bring you back some specimens. You can sometimes find old labels inside scrapbooks in secondhand stores. Look for match books produced by hotels, clubs, charities, airlines, shops, restaurants and other organizations.

Never tear a label off a matchbox.
1. Cut around the **label** with **scissors,** leaving as wide a margin as possible.

2. Put some **cold water** into a **shallow dish.**
Add a **teaspoon of salt** to prevent the colors from running.

3. Place the label face down in the water for ten minutes. If it seems difficult to remove, soak it for a longer time.

4. Peel off the label and place it on **blotting paper** to dry. Then press it between the pages of a **heavy book.**

You can arrange your labels in many different ways – according to the country of origin, the brand name or the design (animals, flags, puzzles, patterns and so on).

Matchbox chest
An ideal way to store your labels is in a matchbox chest.
To make this you will need **six matchboxes.**
1. Take the inside drawer of one matchbox and place it on its end on a sheet of **wrapping paper.** Draw around it six times with a **pencil,** and use **scissors** to cut out these shapes.
2. Stick the paper shapes with **glue** to the fronts of the six matchbox drawers. To make handles, you will need **six brass paper fasteners.** Push one through the center of each drawer front.
3. Lay the matchboxes side by side in pairs and glue the sides together. Place the three pairs on top of one another and glue them in place.
4. With a **ruler,** measure the sides, top and bottom of the chest and cut a strip of paper to just over this size. Coat the chest with glue and wrap the paper around it neatly. Decorate the paper with spare matchbox labels.

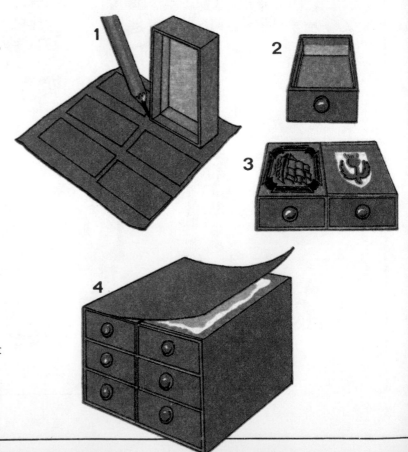

179 ★

Badge bonanza

Many years ago, badges were worn to identify their owners. Today, people still wear them to show that they belong to a certain school, club or profession.
Look for **badges** in cloth, metal and plastic. You can find cloth badges on old uniforms at rummage sales. Junk stores sell military badges in gold, silver and bright colors. Some firms give away badges to advertise themselves.

You may like to wear your collection of badges pinned on to your jacket or even a hat.
You could also display some of your badges on an acoustical ceiling tile. These come in several sizes and you can buy them from a wallpaper store. A gentle push will lodge your badge into position, then you can prop the tile up on a mantelpiece for everyone to see.

180 ★★

Key keeper

Keys and locks vary a lot in their shapes, sizes and patterns. This hobby will start you looking as well as collecting.
Most households have old keys lying around that don't fit anywhere, so start your collection by asking for any spare keys from your own home. (*Don't take keys without first making sure that they are not used.*)
You can also buy old keys and locks very cheaply from junk stores. Don't forget to look for piano keys, keys for furniture, trunks, musical boxes, clocks and padlocks.
When you have a few **keys,** clean them with **metal polish.** Then paint on a coat of **clear polyurethane varnish** with a **small brush.** This keeps the keys shiny.

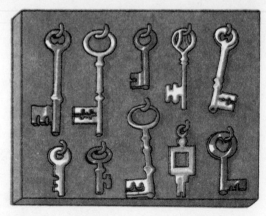

There are many ways to display your keys.
Screw some cup hooks into a board and arrange your collection on the hooks.
Make a mobile from your keys and hang them where they will clink together in the breeze.
Or thread one or two of your prettiest keys on a piece of cord and wear them as a necklace.

181

Double your money

Tell your friends you can double their money!
1. Hide **four coins** inside the pages of a
newspaper. Hold the newspaper so they cannot
fall out.

★ ★ ★ Performance ★ ★ ★

2. Count **four more coins** onto the newspaper
and ask someone to hold out a hand.
3. Tip the coins into the hand, making sure that
the four extra coins from inside the newspaper
fall out too.
Ask your helper to close his hand quickly.
When he opens his hand, he will find he has eight
coins.

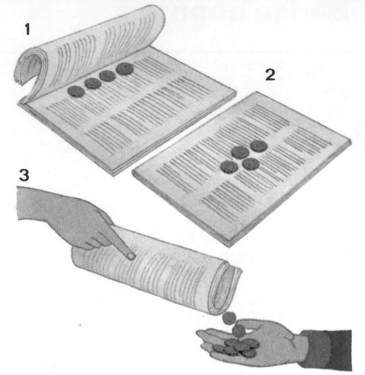

182

Open up

You can get a coin into a bottle without touching
either of them.
Snap a **match** at its center. Do not break it
completely in two.
1. Place the V-shaped match on top of a **bottle.**
Put a **small coin** (smaller than the bottle neck)
on top of the match.

★ ★ ★ Performance ★ ★ ★

2. Drip some **water** from a **sponge** onto the
broken part of the match.
3. The match will move open by itself and let the
coin fall into the bottle.

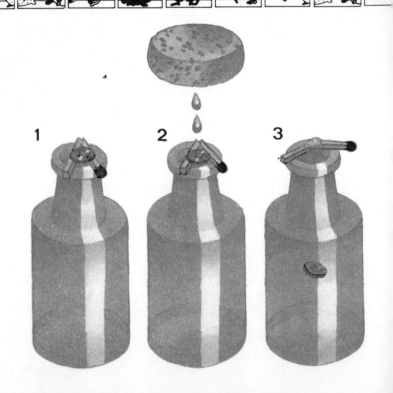

Melting glass

With a little practice, you can appear to pull a ribbon through the bottom of a glass.
With a **needle,** sew 8 inches of **thread** firmly to one end of a **ribbon.**
Tie several knots to make one large knot in the free end of the thread.

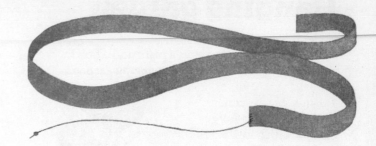

★ ★ ★ ★ ★ ★ ★ ★ ★ ★ ★ **Performance** ★ ★ ★ ★ ★ ★ ★ ★ ★ ★ ★

1. Show your audience a **glass tumbler** and drop the ribbon in it. Make sure that the thread (which is invisible from a distance) is hanging over the edge of the glass.

2. Put a **handkerchief** over the glass. It must be large enough to cover the glass completely.

3. Place a **rubber band** over the rim of the glass (but not too tightly) to hold the handkerchief in position. Put one hand under the handkerchief and pull the thread down. This pulls the ribbon out of the glass.

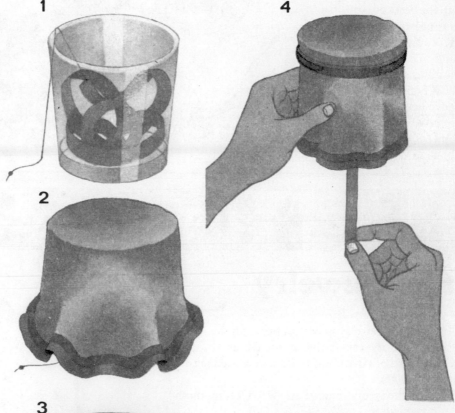

4. Pull the ribbon out from beneath the handkerchief.
It looks as if it has been pulled through the bottom of the glass.

Hanging garden

The top of a carrot serves as a plant and a bowl when you make this miniature hanging garden.

1. Cut a 2 inch section from the top of a **large carrot** with a **knife.** Leave any stalks and shoots attached.

2. Stand the cut end of the carrot on some **absorbent cotton** in a **saucer of water.** Keep the cotton moist and the saucer in sunlight.

3. When the shoots have begun to sprout, remove the carrot top and scoop a hollow bowl in the cut end.

4. Poke a **toothpick** through the top of the bowl. Tie equal lengths of **thread** from each side of the toothpick.

5. Hang up the carrot in a sunny window and fill the bowl with water.

The green shoots of the carrot will grow up to the light, and you will soon have a miniature hanging garden.

Shell jewelry

This kind of jewelry is very popular on the islands of Polynesia in the Pacific Ocean. Collect lots of **tiny shells.** *Make sure the shells are empty first.*

Boil the shells and remove any weed left on them with **tweezers.**

Varnish the best shells with **polyurethane varnish** and a **small brush.**

Ask an adult to help you punch a small hole in the top of each shell with a **strong darning needle.** Gently push and turn the needle until it goes through.

Thread some of the shells on **smooth, lightweight cord** to make necklaces and bracelets. Round and pointy shells look especially attractive together.

Wall flowers

Use some pressed flowers to make a pretty wall hanging. See how to make them in Project 134. Using **scissors,** cut out a rectangular or circular shape from a piece of **cardboard.** Cover the cardboard with **velvet, burlap or linen,** sticking it down at the back with **glue.** Glue some **braid or ribbon** onto the covered cardboard in an oval shape. Tie a bow at the bottom and glue it down.
Inside the oval, glue some **pressed flowers** to make a pretty design.
You can use odd petals to create pictures of other things too. For example, landscapes, gardens, trees or butterflies. Sort the petals into different colors and stick them down to make a collage picture. (Project 24 tells you more about this.)

Dyed egg

Make colored, patterned eggs as gifts for Easter. You can find out how to prepare natural dyes in Project 108.
Slip an **egg** into an **old stocking** with a **flower or leaf** pressed against it.
Prepare some **dye** in an **old saucepan.** Put the egg inside its stocking into the dye and then leave it to soak overnight.
When you take the egg out, the pattern of the leaf or flower will be imprinted on it.

Sweet petals

Make these beautiful, edible flowers and use them to decorate a cake you make.

1

1. Measure six tablespoons of **rose or orangeflower water** (from the druggist) into a **jar.** Add six teaspoons of **crystallized gum arabic** (also from a drugstore) and mix them together.

2

2. Shake the mixture several times in the next two days or until the mixture is completely dissolved. Collect some **small spring flowers,** such as violets, primroses and roses.
Be sure that none of the flowers are poisonous ones.

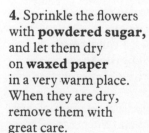

3

3. With a **fine paintbrush,** paint your flowers all over with the gum arabic mixture.

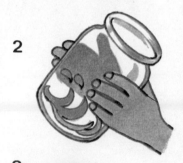

4

4. Sprinkle the flowers with **powdered sugar,** and let them dry on **waxed paper** in a very warm place. When they are dry, remove them with great care.

Cuttlefish lantern

Make a bedroom lamp from cuttlefish shells. You can buy them from pet shops or use other large shells.

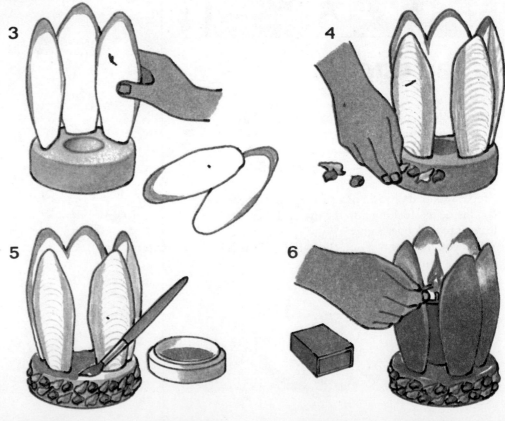

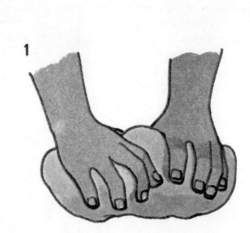

1. Model a circular base about 4 inches across using **self-hardening clay or plasticine.**

2. If you are using clay, push a **wide stubby candle** into it to make a hole.

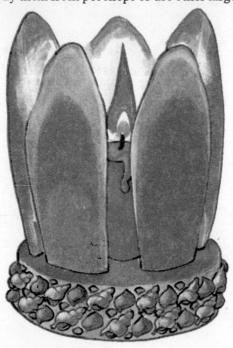

3. Stick the **cuttlefish or other shells** into the clay all around the edge of the base. Leave a space between two of the shells, big enough for your finger to poke a match through.

4. Push some tiny **shells** in around the base for decoration.

5. When the clay is dry, paint the base with **poster colors** and replace the candle.

6. Ask an adult if you can use a **match** to light the candle.

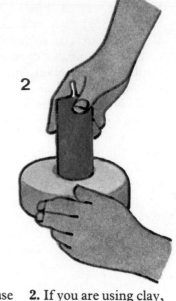

Cushion cover

Transform an old cushion with a bright new cover that you make yourself.

With **scissors,** cut out one large design – a flower perhaps – from **printed fabric.**

Cut two pieces of **plain fabric** the size of your cushion plus 1 inch extra all around.

Pin the design to the right side of one of the plain pieces of fabric. Baste it in place with a **needle** and **thread.**

Sew around the edges of the design in blanket stitch using colored **embroidery thread.**

Remove the basting stitches.

Lay the two fabric pieces right sides together.

Sew around three sides making $\frac{1}{2}$ inch seams.

Turn the cover right side out.

Then put in the cushion and sew up the fourth side.

blanket stitch around the edge of the design

Paper plate mask

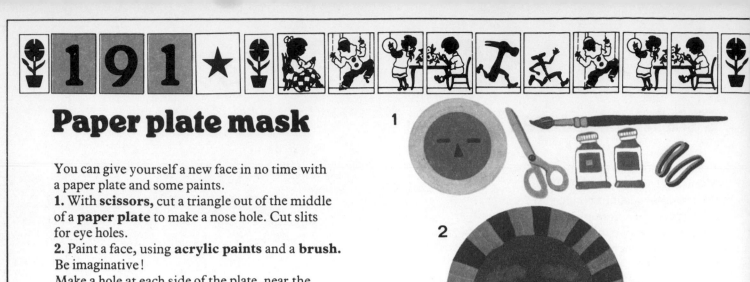

You can give yourself a new face in no time with a paper plate and some paints.

1. With **scissors,** cut a triangle out of the middle of a **paper plate** to make a nose hole. Cut slits for eye holes.

2. Paint a face, using **acrylic paints** and a **brush.** Be imaginative!

Make a hole at each side of the plate, near the edge, using the point of your scissors.

Loop **rubber bands** through the holes, as shown. Slip the bands over your ears and presto! A new you!

Dough beads

Here are bright beads for bright people to make!

1. Crumble three crustless slices of **bread** into a **bowl.**

2. Add three teaspoons of **white glue** and three drops of **dish washing detergent.**

Mix into a smooth dough, adding a little **water** if necessary.

3. Roll little pieces of dough into balls and push them onto a **fine knitting needle.**

Leave them in a warm place for about 24 hours.

4. When the beads are dry, color them with **acrylic paints** and a **brush.**

Thread them onto **shirring elastic** to make a necklace or bracelet.

Flutter butterfly

This butterfly moves and stops still, almost as if it's alive.
First find a **picture of a butterfly** at least 3 inches across in a **magazine or old book.** Or you could draw and color one of your own.

With the point of your **scissors,** make a hole in both ends of a **matchbox drawer** near its base.
1. Ask an adult to cut a **pencil** to fit exactly across the drawer.
Use **household cement** to fix the ends of the pencil to the sides of the drawer. Glue the butterfly to a piece of **thin cardboard.**
Cut out the butterfly and glue it to the bottom of the box.

2. Thread a long piece of thin **string** through the holes at both ends of the drawer.
3. Hold the ends of the string. Tip the string to make the butterfly flutter, and pull it tight to make the butterfly stop. Now make a flock of butterflies!

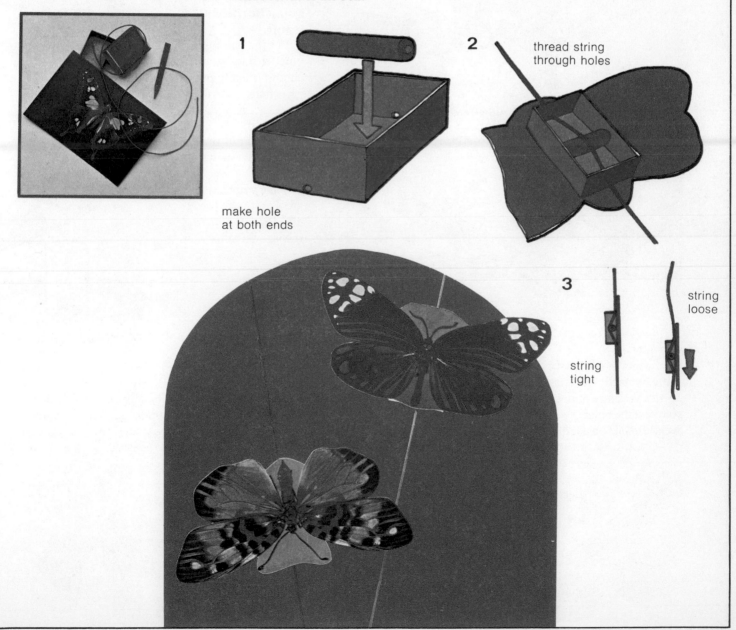

1 make hole at both ends

2 thread string through holes

3 string tight   string loose

Heavy air

Did you know that air is heavy? Even if you can't feel its weight, you can prove it like this.
Put a **ruler** on a table with about 2 inches sticking out over the edge.
1. Tap the end lightly with your hand. The ruler will fly off the table.

2. Put the ruler on the table again and this time cover it with a sheet of **newspaper.**
Tap the end lightly with your hand. The ruler will not move.

The paper is too light to hold the ruler on the table by itself. But the paper itself is held down by the pressure of the air above it. When you try to move the ruler, you have to overcome the weight of air on a large surface.

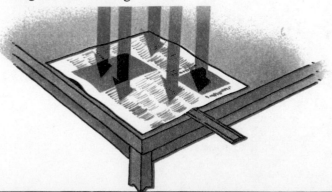

 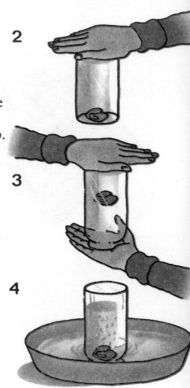

Powder power

Why does baking powder make a cake rise? Do this experiment and you can see how it works.

1. Put about three teaspoons of **baking powder** in the middle of a **paper tissue.** Fold up the paper to make a small bundle.

Fill a **narrow jar or small bottle** with **water.**
2. Put the baking powder bundle into the jar and quickly put your hand over the top.

3. Turn the jar upside down and put the top into a **bowl of water.**

4. Take your hand away from the top. The level of water in the jar will fall.

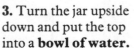

The water goes through the tissue and dissolves the baking powder. The baking powder gives off gas which forces water out of the jar. When you make a cake with baking powder, the gas given off during cooking helps the cake rise.

Slave magnet

Some interesting things happen when you do this experiment. It looks complicated, but persevere! Strip the plastic covering from the ends of **two pieces of electrical wire,** each about 1 yard long.

1. Connect one end of a piece of wire to one terminal of a **battery.** Connect the other end of the wire to one of the screws in a **light bulb holder.** Now fix one end of the second piece of wire to the second screw in the bulb holder, leaving the other end loose.

2. Tie a piece of **thread** to the middle of a small **magnet** so that it hangs straight. Tie the other end of the thread to one end of a **ruler,** or fix it with **cellophane tape.**

3. Sandwich the other end of the ruler between some **books** so that the bottom of the magnet hangs about $\frac{1}{4}$ inch above a table. Lay the wire connecting the battery to the bulb holder so that it runs in a straight line under the magnet. Make sure that it lies flat.

4. Now touch the other battery terminal with the end of the loose wire and take it off again. The magnet will swing around as soon as the light comes on. If you touch the battery with the wire and make the light flash slowly on and off you can get the magnet to turn around and around.

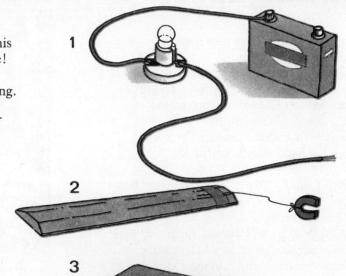

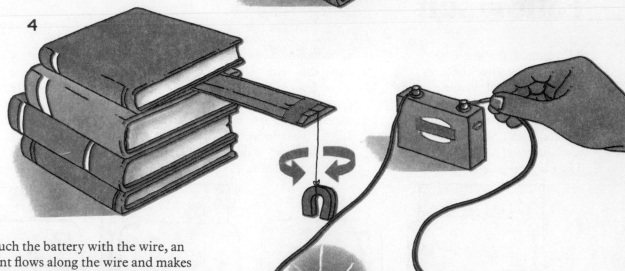

When you touch the battery with the wire, an electric current flows along the wire and makes the light come on. The same current also creates a magnetic field around the wire. This magnetic field makes the magnet move. An electric motor works in a similar way.

Sign language

This is a good game to play on a trip since you don't need any equipment.
Two players face each other with one hand behind their backs. After counting three, they show their hands in one of these positions:
—a closed fist stands for "stone"
—two fingers extended stands for "scissors"
—an open flat hand stands for "paper."

If one player shows "paper" and the other shows "scissors," "scissors" scores one point because scissors can cut paper.
If you show "paper" and "stone" together, "paper" wins a point because paper can wrap a stone.
If you show "scissors" and "stone," "stone" wins a point because a stone can blunt scissors.
If both players show the same, they both score.

Follow suit

This game is for two or more players using a deck of cards.
Divide a **deck of playing cards** equally among the players.
Players sort their cards into *suits* (hearts, diamonds, clubs, spades) and *sequences* (Ace to King).
The player who is holding the seven of diamonds plays first by putting down this card.
The player on the left must try to place the six or the eight of diamonds above or below the seven. If the player does not hold either of these cards, he or she puts down the seven of another suit.

If the player holds none of these cards, he or she must pass and the player on the left continues.
In this way, each player in turn adds to the top or bottom of any of the four sequences.
The player who uses up all his or her cards first is the winner.

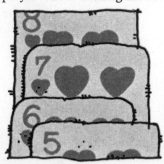

What's wrong?

How observant are you? You can find out by playing this game.

Choose a room to play in, then **ask an adult** to remove all breakable objects before you start.

Everyone looks around the room and tries to remember as much about it as possible.

Everyone goes out of the room except one person. The person left behind changes one thing in the room – hides a cushion, moves an ornament or draws a curtain, for example.

The other players return. The winner is the one who notices "what's wrong" first.

The winner stays in the room to make another change, and the game continues.

Ring-a-pin

This is a good game for a summer party since it's best played out-of-doors.

Find or buy some **small prizes** (cheap toys and bags of candy). Attach them to a **clothesline** with **clothespins,** or if you can't pin them easily, tie them to short pieces of **string** first. Give each player six **cardboard rings** and ask them to stand two or three yards away from the line. They should then try to throw the rings over the pins. If a player manages to ring a pin, he or she gets the prize attached to it.

Apple bobbing

This ancient game is traditionally played on Halloween night.

Fill a **bucket or bowl** with **water** and then put in five or six **apples.**

Tie the first player's hands loosely behind his or her back with a **scarf or a piece of string.** The player should kneel down in front of the bucket and try to pick up as many apples as possible with his or her teeth. Allow a set time (say two minutes) before the next player takes a turn.

The winner is the player who manages to get the most apples out of the bucket in the given time. You could also bob for marshmallows which are suspended on cotton thread from the ceiling!

Button booty

Clothes wear out long before buttons do, so there are always plenty of spare ones to collect. You can find interesting ones in junk shops, markets and at rummage sales – but ask to look in the button box at home first.

You might like to collect only one type of button – for example, buttons from uniforms (the armed forces or any uniformed service), buttons made from a particular material (glass, wood, metal or plastic), or decorative buttons or old buttons. Here is a way of displaying your buttons to their best advantage.

1. With **scissors,** cut out a piece of **colored felt** the same size as the **lid of a cardboard shoe box.**

1

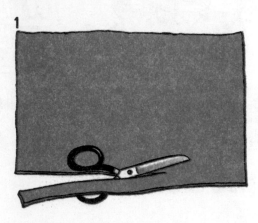

2. Arrange your **buttons** on the felt to make a design or a picture. Then sew each button into place using a **needle** and **thread.**

2

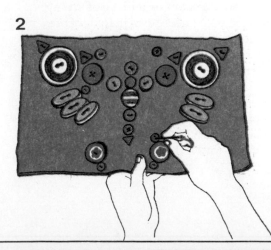

3. Spread a thin layer of **glue** all over the lid of the box, and place your picture carefully into position. Smooth it down from the middle outward, making sure there are no creases.

3

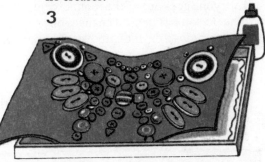

While your picture is drying, make a support for it.

4. Cut a strip of **cardboard** from the rest of the shoe box almost as long as your picture. Make a fold about a third of the way down. Cover this section with glue and stick it roughly in the middle of the back of your picture, as shown.

4

If you prefer, you can make two holes on both sides of the top of the lid, thread some string through it, and hang it up.

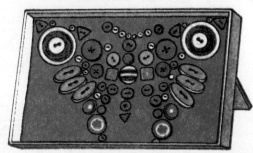

Pocket teaser

This teaser is fun to make and fun to play with after you have made it.

Find a **small box with a transparent lid** (a cheese box perhaps) and **four wooden beads, small dried beans or cake decorating balls.** Put the box on a piece of **cardboard** and then draw around it with a **pencil.** Cut out the shape with **scissors.** Make sure that the cardboard fits snugly into the base of the box.

Paint a face, landscape or pattern on the cardboard with **poster paints.**

With the point of your scissors, carefully poke four holes in the picture. They should be just big enough for the beads or balls to sit in without falling out too easily.

Fix the painted cardboard into the base of the box with **glue.** Put in the beads or balls and glue on the lid. Now you can play with your pocket teaser. Try to get all the balls into the holes in the shortest possible time. Time yourself with a watch to see how expert you can become.

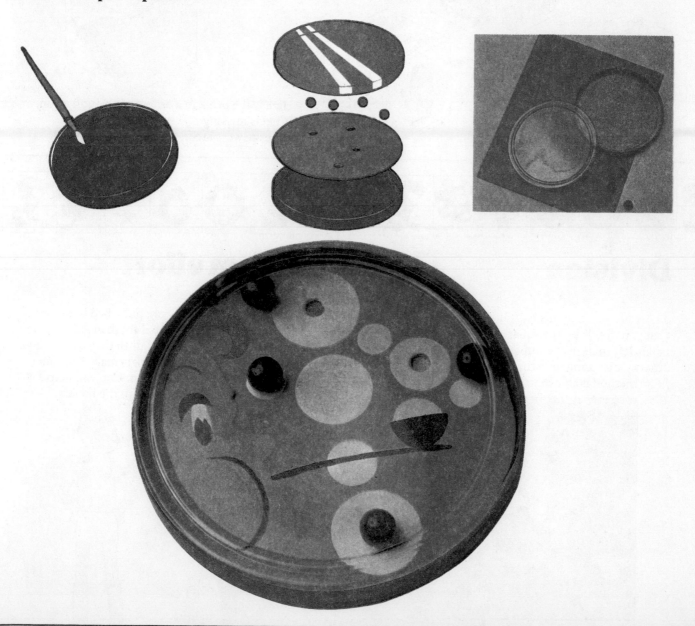

Batty bricks

Here are three drawings of the same brick in different positions. The brick has a different picture on each of its sides.
They are:
—an airplane
—a hand
—a tree
—a rabbit
—a butterfly
—a bird

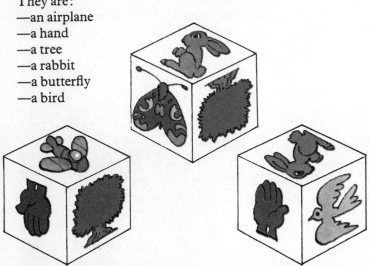

Here is the same brick in two different positions, but with one picture missing in each case. What should those pictures be? (These are easy.)

Here is the brick in a different position again. What is missing now? (This is harder.)
(The answers are in the back of the book.)

Division

There are seven tennis balls inside this square. Can you divide up the square so that each tennis ball is left in its own compartment without any others – but using only three straight lines? (The method is shown in the back of the book.)

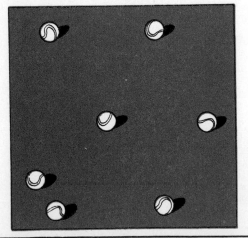

Team effort

These two boys are being punished because they had a fight during a school football game.
They have to stay behind until they can arrange themselves so that their shirts make a number that can be divided by seven. Can you help? (The solution is in the back of the book.)

Remember the date

This is a drawing of King Henry VIII who ruled England and Wales in the 16th century. Can you see something that should not be in the picture? (Check your answer in the back of the book.)

Camp cooking

Cooking outside is great fun, in the chilly winter, the autumn dusk or on a summer evening. **Ask an adult** to help you whenever you light a fire. *Never* light a fire near anything that could catch fire and *always* make sure the fire is completely out when you are finished.

Wrap some whole, unskinned **potatoes** in **aluminum foil.** Push them under the hot ashes of the **fire** with a **stick,** making sure they are well covered. Test them with a **skewer** to find out when they are soft and cooked. Then remove the foil, slice open the potatoes and eat them with butter or cheese. Spear some frankfurters on **long toasting forks,** and grill them over the glowing flames.

Toast **marshmallows** on the end of a toasting fork until they are soft and gooey.

Surprise sprouts

Help the family budget by growing your own curly bean sprouts for a meal.

1. Put a handful of **green mung beans** into a **jar.** Cover the top of the jar with a piece of **muslin or cheesecloth.** Keep it in place with a **rubber band.**

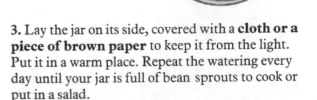

2. Through the muslin, pour enough **water** to cover the beans and wet them all thoroughly. Pour the water out again through the top.

3. Lay the jar on its side, covered with a **cloth or a piece of brown paper** to keep it from the light. Put it in a warm place. Repeat the watering every day until your jar is full of bean sprouts to cook or put in a salad.

Leaf skeletons

Leaf skeletons are good for decorating cards or calendars, or you could make a collection of them for their own sake.

Collect together as many **differently-shaped broad leaves** as you can find.

Ask an adult to help you use the **stove.** Half fill a **saucepan** with **water** and add a tablespoon of **washing soda.**

1. Heat the water until it is nearly boiling. Then add your leaves. Simmer them gently for about an hour or until the leafy part begins to come away from the leaf spines.

Take the leaves off the heat and let them cool.

2. Brush the soft parts away from the spines completely, using a soft **brush** and a gentle touch.

3. Put the leaf skeletons into a solution of water with a teaspoon of **bleach** for one hour.

Then rinse them gently under the cold tap.

Seeds to see

Make beautiful pictures from seeds that you have gathered yourself.

1. Collect **apple, melon, watermelon, corn** and **pumpkin seeds** and some **dried peas.** Make sure they are clean and dry. Paint some of the seeds with clear **polyurethane varnish** and a **brush.** With a **pencil,** draw a design on a piece of colored **cardboard.** Simple geometric designs work best.

2. Use **glue** to stick the seeds onto your design in bands of contrasting colors.

3. You can make a border for your seed picture by gluing **braid or rope** around the edge. Fix a **picture hanger** on the back and hang your seed picture up where everyone can see it.

Tame iceberg

Learn to lift an ice cube without touching it.
(Project 62 tells you how to carry out an
experiment with ice cubes.)
Ask a friend to try to lift an ice cube out of
a glass of water with a piece of string, without
touching the ice. Your friend won't be able to
do it, but you will.

★★★★ Performance ★★★★

Put an **ice cube** in a **glass of water**.
1. Lay one end of a piece of **string** on top of
the ice cube.

1

2. Pour some **salt** on the ice cube and the string.
Wait a few seconds and then lift the string up.

2

3. The ice cube will stick to the string and
can be lifted from the glass.

3

Vanishing woman

Make a woman mysteriously appear and disappear
in a picture frame.

1. With a **pencil,** draw **1**
a woman in a frame and
an empty frame onto
two pieces of **thin
cardboard** the size of
your hand. Color them
with **felt-tipped pens.**

2. Fold the two cards **2**
in half. Using **glue,**
stick one fold of each
of the two halves
together, as shown.

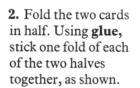

3. With **scissors,** cut a **3**
third piece of cardboard
the same size as the
other two. Glue it to
the back of the two
folded cards.

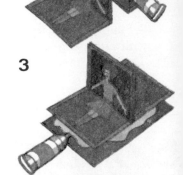

★★★★ Performance ★★★★

4. Hold up the card **4**
with the flap up,
showing the woman in
the picture frame.

5. Now pass your hand **5**
over the cardboard and
secretly lower the
flap.

6. Presto! Your **6**
audience will see an
empty picture frame.

Match mend

This is an easy trick to perform, but your audience will be amazed.

1. Find a **handkerchief with a hem.** Push a **matchstick** into it.

★★★★ **Performance** ★★★★

2. Show your audience **another matchstick** and then wrap it up in the handkerchief.

3. Break the matchstick inside the hem of the hanky. Your audience will hear you breaking it and will think you are breaking the matchstick you have just shown them.

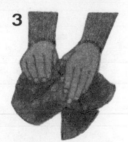

4. Open the handkerchief and show that the matchstick is whole again.

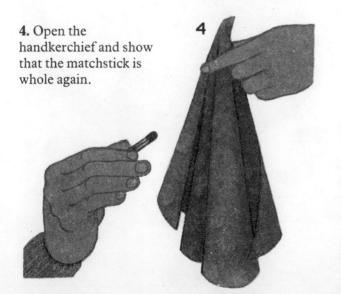

Patriotic paper

Make your friends think you can turn a few colored ribbons into a British flag.

1. Fold up a **small flag** and put it on a sheet of **newspaper.**
Put another sheet of newspaper on top of the first sheet with the flag.

2. With **glue,** stick the edges of the two sheets together so that the flag is hidden.

★★★★ **Performance** ★★★★

Find **two or three ribbons** in the same colors as your flag.
3. Show the ribbons to your audience and then wrap them in the prepared newspaper.

4. Tear open the top of the newspaper parcel and pull out the flag. Make sure your audience doesn't see the ribbons!

216

Shuttlecock

Don't wait to be given a set of shuttlecocks. It's more fun to make your own and they work just as well.

Use the fine side of a **kitchen grater** to shave one end of a **large cork** into a rounded shape. Shorten **eight feathers** to a length of 2½ inches by trimming the quill ends with **scissors.** Push the shortened feathers into the top of the cork all around the edge. They should bend slightly outward.

Ask a friend to stand on the other side of a wash line or low tree branch. Bat the shuttlecock back and forth with your hands. Score a penalty every time you miss the shuttlecock or it doesn't get over the "net."

2½ ins

217

Tin can drums

Beat out the rhythms of your favorite tunes on these mini-drums. Use **pencils** as drumsticks.

Find **three empty tin cans** – a short fat one, a tall thin one and one in between.
1. Use a **paintbrush** and **acrylic paints** to paint all the cans.

Stretch **three balloons** by blowing them up, and then letting out the air again.
2. With **scissors,** cut the balloons in half across their widest part.

Stretch a piece of balloon over the top of each can and hold them on with **rubber bands.**
3. Wind **masking tape** around the three cans to hold them together.

1

2

3

Fish mobiles

You can make these strange fish into a mobile or you can use them to decorate a bare wall.

With **scissors,** cut some different fish shapes out of **colored paper.** Flatten some **drinking straws.** Curl some around a **pencil** and fold others into zigzags. Cut one long edge of some of them with **pinking shears** (scissors with serrated blades).

Cut some straws into short lengths to make rings. With a **paintbrush** and **poster paints,** paint some of the straws and straw pieces in different colors.

Arrange the straws in varying designs on the paper fish. Stick them in place with **glue.**

To make a mobile, thread different lengths of **thread** through the tops of the fishes with a **needle.** Knot the thread securely. Then tie the other ends of the threads to a **coat hanger.** Hang your mobile from the ceiling or the top of a window frame.

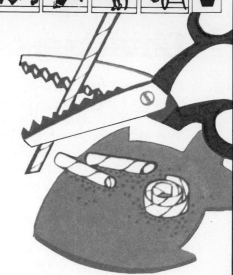

Dewdrops

Discover why dew appears on a summer morning.
Put a **glass jar** in the **refrigerator** for about
30 minutes. Fill **another jar** with **hot water.**
After a few minutes, empty it and dry it inside
and out with a **dish towel.** Take the cold jar
out of the refrigerator and dry it well.
Put both jars in a steamy room, such as a
kitchen or bathroom. The cold jar will become
moist and the warm jar will stay dry.
This happens because warm air can hold more
water vapor than cold air. When warm air meets
a cold surface, such as the cold jar, some of
the vapor *condenses* (or beomes liquid). In
the same way, water vapor in the summer air
condenses into dew when it meets cold ground.

Ink blot

There's more to ink than meets the eye! Prove
it by doing this simple experiment.
Put a drop of **black ink** on a strip of **blotting
paper.** It's best to use a **fountain pen** for this.
Dip one end of the blotting paper into a **bowl** of
cold **water** and leave it for a few minutes.
As the water rises up the blotting paper, the
ink will separate into a series of colored
bands. Take the paper out of the water and let
it dry so that you can see the different dyes
and chemicals that make up black ink.
Years ago, people had to mix all these
ingredients together by hand to make ink.

Straw chimney

By doing this experiment, you can find out why
fire goes up a chimney and not into the room
where the fire is.

Half fill a **glass jar** with **water.**
1. Add some **cold tea or coffee** to color the
water. Put a **drinking straw** in the water.

1

2. Hold the jar and the straw, and stand in
front of a **mirror.**
Hold the straw and put your lips against it
just below the top. Blow strongly over the top
of the straw.

2

3. Look in the mirror and you will see the
water rise in the straw as you blow.

3

As you blow, the force of air from your mouth
pulls air out of the straw. This makes a space
in the straw (called a *vacuum*) which is then
filled by the water.
Chimneys work in a similar way. When the wind
blows, it sucks the smoke from the fire up the
chimney and out into the open air.

Deep-sea diver

You can make the little diver go up and down in a jar of water without even touching it.

1. Using **tracing paper** and a **pencil,** trace the diver onto **thick cardboard.** Color it with **felt-tipped pens.** Cover the picture on both sides with **cellophane tape** to make it waterproof. Cut out the diver with **scissors.**

2

Press a small lump of **plasticine** onto the diver's back.
2. Press a **pen top** into the plasticine as shown. The open end of the pen top must point downward.

3. Fill a **glass jar** with **water** and push the diver in. If it floats, you need to add more plasticine. If it sinks, you need less. Make adjustments until the diver sinks and rises slowly when pushed gently.

Cut a **round balloon** in half so that you can open it out into one flat sheet.
4. Stretch the flat balloon over the jar. Ask a friend to put a **rubber band** around the balloon to hold it tightly in place.

5. To make the diver move up and down, press the rubber top down with the tips of your fingers, and then let go slowly. The pressure of your hand forces water into the pen top: the diver gets heavier, and sinks. When you remove your hand, water is sucked out, so the diver rises again.

Don't be last

Don't be deceived by this game – it looks easy,
but there is a secret to winning it!
Only two players can compete in this game.
Lay out **15 matchsticks** side by side on a table.
Taking turns, each player picks up one,
two or three matchsticks, but no more.
Keep picking up the matchsticks until there is
only one left. (Make sure that it's your
opponent that picks it up, not you!)
Whoever picks up the very last matchstick is
the loser of the game.

Hear! Hear!

Noises often sound quite strange when you
cannot see what is making them.
Collect some **objects which make recognizable
noises** – for example, a can of soda,
water to pour from a pitcher into a bowl, a clock
to wind, some paper to tear. **Ask an adult** to
help you find these things. You will also need
paper and pencils for all the players.
Choose one player to sit out of sight behind a
screen or sofa. The hidden player should
then make noises with one object at a time.
The other players try to recognize the sounds
and write down the names of the objects making
them. The player who has the most correct
answers is the winner.

Stick-in-the-mud

This is an energetic game that will warm you up
on a cold day or keep you outside on a hot one.
The more players you have for this game, the
better. One player is chosen as "It." "It"
must chase the others and tag them by touching
them on the shoulder. The players who are
tagged must stand still, with their legs apart
and their arms outstretched, calling for help.
Any players who have not been caught can
release them by crawling through their legs.
To speed up the game when there are a lot of
players, more than one "It" should be chosen.
The game is over when all the players except
one are "stuck-in-the-mud." The player who
has managed not to be caught then becomes "It."

Sniper

Here's a game to play with marbles.
Place **ten to 15 marbles** in a circle, with one
marble in the center. There should be plenty
of space between each marble.
Using **string or chalk,** mark out a "shooting
line" about 3 yards away from the circle.
Taking turns, the players must try to hit
the center marble with their "shooters." If
anyone hits any of the other marbles or fails
to hit the center marble, that player must leave
his or her shooter where it is. If the player
succeeds in hitting the center marble, he or she
can then try to hit any of the other marbles,
including those left behind by players who have
shot before. He or she can keep any marbles hit
after hitting the center marble. The player who
collects the most marbles wins the game.

227 ★

Chinese whispers

This is a good game for a party, especially when everyone is tired out at the end.

All the players sit in a long line. The person at the end of the line thinks of a short message and whispers it to the player sitting next in line. The message is passed along in this way until it reaches the other end of the line. The last player at the end of the line calls out the message he or she has received. The first player calls out the sentence originally thought up and the two are compared.

The message can be as silly or serious as you like. But one thing you can be certain of – by the time it's traveled all the way down the line, it will be something quite different!

228 ★

Snail race

Snails usually come out at night to feed on plants and leaves. But you can often find them in damp places during the day, especially in the autumn when they feed on rotting leaves. Collect as many **snails** as you can find. Using **poster paints,** mark a different number on each snail's back. With a piece of **chalk,** draw a circle on a suitable piece of ground outside. Put all the snails in the center of the circle. The first one to cross the chalk line wins.

Bottle tops

Bottle tops come in all sorts of bright colors, some plain and some with trade names. Look for them in candy stores and anywhere else that sells drinks.

To display your **bottle tops,** sew a wide hem around a piece of **cloth,** using a **needle** and **thread.**

Pull out the disk from inside each of the bottle tops. Put the disk on one side of the cloth and the top on the other, as shown. Press the disk back into the top, over the cloth, so that it fits firmly inside. Use as many tops as you need to make an attractive design.

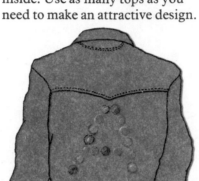

Pass **two bamboo or cane rods** through the top and bottom hems of the cloth. Tie **string** to both sides of one rod and hang up your display on a wall.

If you **ask an adult** first, you could decorate your jeans or a jacket with spare bottle tops.

Fossil finds

Fossils are the remains or traces of plants or animals which lived millions of years ago. A dinosaur skeleton is a fossil and so is the imprint (or impression) of a tiny fern.

It's very unlikely that you would ever discover a dinosaur skeleton, but you might find smaller fossils by searching on cliffs and among rocks by the seashore.

Look for imprints of patterned shells, or for *ammonites* (spirally-coiled fossils of extinct sea creatures) and *trilobites* (the fossil ancestors of lobsters, crayfish and shrimps).

If the **fossil** is too big to carry home, press a lump of **plasticine** over it to get an impression. At home, make a plaster of Paris cast of the impression in the plasticine. (Project 6 shows you how to do this.)

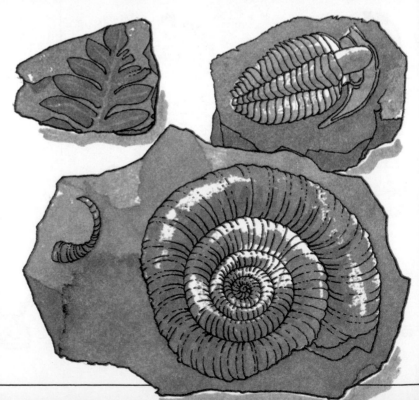

Paper book

You can make a fascinating collection of paper: there's silver paper, colored cellophane, tissue paper, decorated wrapping paper and many more kinds. A good way to display them is to make a "sample book."

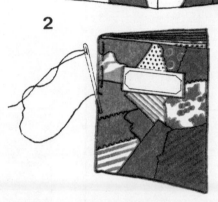

Using **scissors,** cut all your pieces of **paper** to an equal size. Cut some **thin cardboard** to double that size.
1. Fold the cardboard down the center to make a cover. Decorate it by sticking on bits of paper with **glue.**

Slip your collection of papers inside the cover, making sure all the pages are in line.
2. With a **needle** and **thread,** sew firmly down the spine of the book.

Mementos

Mementos are the little things which remind you of special occasions in your life. A theater program, a ticket from a museum or a nature park, a menu, or even a paper party hat can remind you of the fun you had long after the event has passed.
The Victorians used to glue their mementos into a big scrapbook called a "commonplace book." You could do the same, or you could keep your **personal mementos** – including letters, photographs and cards – in a memento box.

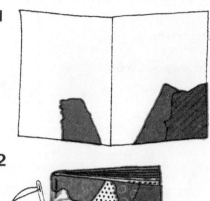

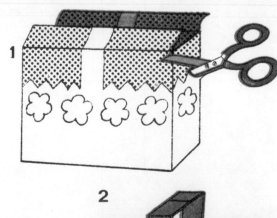

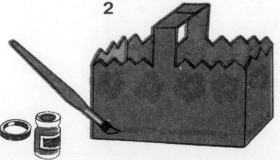

Cut a strip of **plain paper** large enough to cover a **cereal box** and stick it on with **glue.** Draw a jagged line across the box with a **pencil,** as shown.
1. With **scissors,** cut away the shaded area, leaving handles as shown in the diagram. Glue the two handle strips together.
2. Use **poster paint** and a **paintbrush** to decorate the basket.

Crazy cutouts

Somebody has cut out six crazy shapes from this sheet of paper. Can you decide which shape fits into which hole?
(Try tracing and cutting out the shapes if you can't fit them right away.)

Rectangles

With **scissors,** cut out four rectangular pieces of **paper** and arrange them as in the drawing. By moving only one piece of paper, can you make a square? Watch out! There's a trick to this.

(The arrangement is shown on the pages of Answers in the back of the book.)

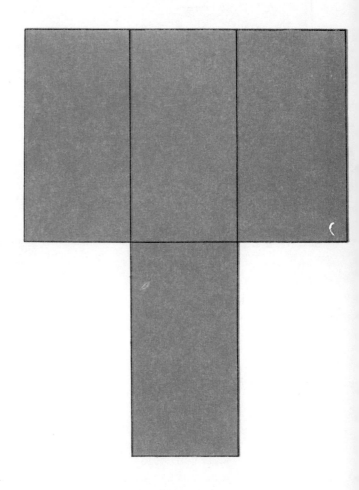

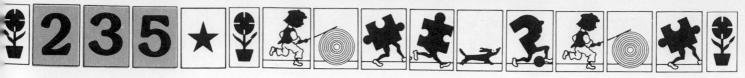

Witchery

Here are two pictures of a witch and her cat riding a strange machine. The pictures look identical, but there are 23 differences between them. Can you spot all the differences?

Miniature museum

Have you ever thought of running your own museum? Collecting and preparing your **exhibits** is a fascinating pastime, and you are doubly rewarded when your family and friends come to visit it.
Everything you find in fields, gardens and by the seashore can be good material for a museum.
When your parents or neighbors dig in their gardens, look for old bottles, crockery and coins.
You could find fossils in rocks by the seashore. (See Project 230.)
If you live near a river, try mud-larking – combing the muddy banks for treasure. At the seashore, look for driftwood, shells, pebbles and dried strands of seaweed.

After sorting and cleaning all your finds, mount them on **cards,** using **glue or cellophane tape.** Write notes on each card, describing where and when you found the exhibit and what it is.
If you find something especially interesting and want to know more about it, take it to your local museum and ask the *curator* (the person who takes care of the museum) to look at it. You might have found something rare!
If you find animal or bird bones, first try to identify them. **Ask an adult** to help you clean the bones. Boil them in an **old saucepan** until all the flesh is removed.
Soak them overnight in a

pint of **water** mixed with one teaspoon of **bleach.** Rinse the bones well and dry them slowly. If you like, you can make the bones shiny by painting with **polyurethane varnish.**

Green hair

Here's a way to give your Halloween pumpkin a fine head of hair.

1. Ask an adult to cut the top off a **pumpkin** with a **knife.** Scoop out some of the flesh, but be careful not to break into the soft center.

2. Line the hollow in the pumpkin with a layer of **moist absorbent cotton.**

3. Sow **grass or mustard and watercress seeds** on the moist cotton. Keep it watered until the head has a crop of green hair. Then cut out the features of your pumpkin head for Halloween.

Seaweed slides

Here's a different way to remember your vacation by the sea.

1. Collect various kinds of **seaweed** in a **bucket.** Keep the seaweed fresh in **seawater** until you are ready to use it.

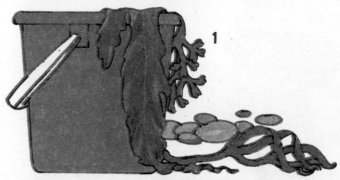

2. Buy some **35mm slide mounts.** (They are cheap and easily available at your local photo supply store.)

Cut your seaweed to size with **scissors.**
3. Open the mounts and place pieces of seaweed between them. Arrange them in attractive patterns, leaving space around each piece.

You will enjoy looking at your seaweed slides as much as your vacation snapshots. If you know anyone with a **slide projector,** you could **ask an adult** to project the slides. This will show the beautiful shapes and colors of the seaweed to their best advantage.

Goodbye container

With a little practice, you can make a container vanish in front of your audience's eyes.

1. Using **household cement,** stick a **yogurt container** to the middle of a sheet of **stiff cardboard** so that it looks like a cup on a tray.

1

2. Bend a piece of **fuse wire** into a circle the same size as the top of the container.

2

3. Using a **needle** and **thread,** sew the wire circle onto the center of a **handkerchief.**

3

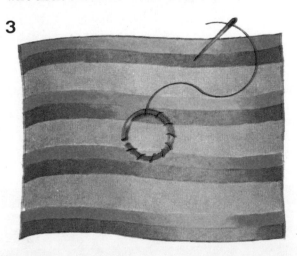

★ ★ ★ ★ **Performance** ★ ★ ★ ★

4. Show your audience the cup on the tray, and then cover it with the handkerchief.

4

5. Lift the handkerchief up a little by holding the wire circle through the cloth. It will look as though you are holding the container.

5

At the same time, turn the tray over so that the container is hidden behind it. Then lean the tray against a **wall or box** on your table, making sure the container cannot be seen.

6. Shake the handkerchief – and your audience will see that the container has vanished.

6

Wobbly pencil

This trick will probably surprise you as much as your audience – and it's very easy, too.

Hold one end of a **long pencil** lightly between the tips of your fingers.
Move your hand up and down quickly to make the pencil move.
The pencil will wobble and look as though it is made of rubber.

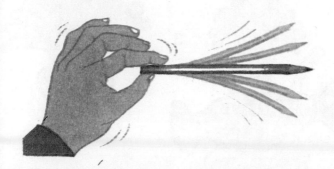

Name the name

No need to practice this trick – just look confident and your friends will think you've turned into a genius!

Tear up some **paper** into slips, and ask your audience to call out different names.
With a **pen**, write just one of the names on all the slips of paper. Your audience will believe you are writing down each of the different names as they are called out. Put all the slips of paper into a **box with a lid,** and shake the box.
Ask someone to take out one slip of paper, but tell them not to show it to you. Throw away all the other slips of paper.
Now you can tell everyone the name on the slip of paper!

Ring the changes

For this trick, you need to wear a **jacket with pockets and wide sleeves.**

Find **two plastic bangle bracelets,** exactly the same and big enough to fit over your arm.
Put one of the bangles over your hand and push it a little way up your sleeve and out of sight.

★★★★ **Performance** ★★★★

1. Hand someone a length of **rope** and ask him or her to tie the ends to each of your wrists.
Show your audience the second plastic bangle.
Then turn around for a moment.

2. Put the plastic bangle you showed into your pocket. Pull the first bangle down from your sleeve and onto the rope.

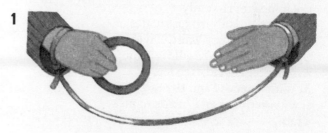

3. When you turn back to face your audience, they will think they see the bangle you showed them hanging on the rope.

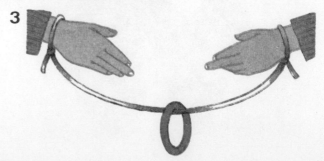

Yarn dolls

You've probably seen corn dolls.
Now try making them out of yarn.
Wind **thick yarn** around and
around the *length* of a **postcard** to
make a thick sausage shape.
Slip the yarn off the card. Tie
the bundle in two places near the
top to make the face.

1. With **scissors,** cut through all
the loops at the top and bottom.
Wind yarn around the *width* of the
card to make the arms.
Slip it off the card and tie each
end of the bundle. Snip through
the loops. Push the arms through
the middle of the body.

2. Tie a piece of yarn just under
the arms to make a waist. Divide
the bottom of the bundle in half
to make legs. Bind each leg.

3. With a **needle** and **thread**
sew on **sequins** and **beads** to make
a face.

Mirror image

Paint half a painting and end up with a whole one!

Fold a sheet of **paper** in half.

1. Paint half a picture on one half of the paper, using **thick poster paint.** Choose a subject that is *symmetrical* (made up of two identical halves) like a face, an apple, a butterfly or a leaf. Make sure the center of the design lies along the fold in the paper.

2. Quickly fold the unpainted half of the paper on top of the painted half and press your hand down on it firmly.

3. Carefully open out the paper. You now have a symmetrical painting, with one side exactly mirroring the other.

Vertical test

If you make a *plumb line* (a line with a weight on the end) you can see whether things are *vertical* (straight up and down).

Find 2 yards of **thin string**. Tie a **paper clip** to one end. Hold a **pebble** or **small stone** on the paper clip, and mold a lump of **plasticine** around them both.

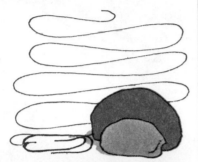

Use a **thumbtack** to fix the string to the top of a **door frame** with the door open. Wait until the plumb line stops swinging.

If there is a big gap between the frame and the bottom of the plumb line, the frame is not vertical – it is leaning inward.

Nor is it vertical if the plumb line hangs across it – the frame is leaning outward. When you hang pictures in your room, use the plumb line to check that the picture frames are straight.

On the level

A *carpenter's level* is used for checking that surfaces are *horizontal* (level with the horizon). Here's one that's easy to make.

Put some **cold coffee or tea** in a **glass jar**. Put the jar on the edge of a **table**. Suspend a **plumb line** next to the jar, but without touching it. The side of the jar should be parallel with the plumb line. (Put paper under the jar to level it, if necessary.) Fix **colored plastic tape** so that it is exactly on the line made by the surface of the liquid.

Now if you put the jar on a surface that is not horizontal, the liquid will not line up with the edge of the colored tape.

Circular exercise

This project shows how to draw a circle without using a compass. You need a steady hand, so practice a little if you don't draw a perfect circle the first time you try.

Put a sheet of **paper** on a piece of **very thick cardboard.**

Push a **thumbtack** into the paper and cardboard. The thumbtack should be firmly fixed without going right through the cardboard.

Tie two ends of a length of **string** together to make a loop. The loop should not be longer than the width of your sheet of paper.

Put the string loop around the thumbtack.

Hold a **pencil** upright inside the loop.

Keeping the string taut, carefully move the pencil around the thumbtack to make a circle.

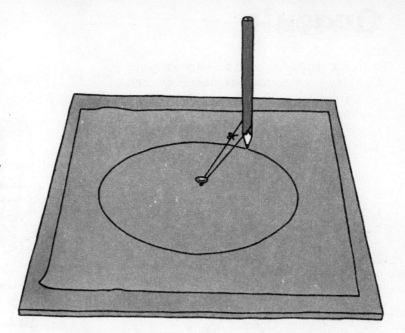

Loopy oval

By using a string loop, you can also draw a perfect oval. The method is very similar to drawing a circle, but you need **two thumbtacks** instead of one.

Put a sheet of **paper** on a piece of **very thick cardboard.**

Fix the two thumbtacks, a little way apart, into the paper and cardboard. Be careful not to push the thumbtacks right through the cardboard.

Knot the ends of a length of **string** to make a loop shorter than the width of your paper.

Put the string loop around both thumbtacks.

Hold a **pencil** upright inside the loop.

Keeping the string taut, move the pencil around the thumbtacks to get an oval.

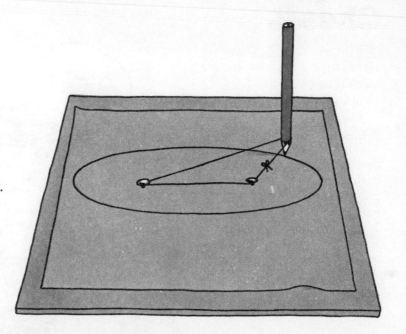

Queenie

This is a very old, though well-known game. One player is chosen to be Queenie. Queenie stands with his or her back to the other players, holding a **ball**.

Queenie throws the ball over his or her shoulder and all the other players compete to catch it. They then form a line, holding their hands behind their backs. One of them will be holding the ball.

Queenie can then turn around, and must try to guess who is holding the ball. The others can make it as difficult as possible by acting as if they have the ball.

If Queenie guesses correctly, the same player remains in place and the game starts again. If Queenie is wrong, the person holding the ball becomes the new Queenie.

Cheats

Here's a game in which you are actually meant to cheat.

Deal out a **deck of playing cards** among all the players. The first player to the left of the dealer who has an ace places it face-down on the table, calling "One!" as the card is discarded. The next player puts down a two of any suit, and calls out "Two!"

If the player does not have a two, he or she puts down another card and still calls out "Two!"

The next player does the same, calling out "Three!", and so on.

At any stage during the game, one player can challenge another by calling out "Cheat!" The player who has been accused must then turn up his or her card.

If the accusation is correct, all the players give the accused player one of their cards.

If the accusation is false, the accused player gives one card to the accuser.

Then the game continues as before, until one of the players has no cards left. This player is the winner.

Animal voices

This is a game to warm everyone up at a party.
One player is chosen to be "It."
It leaves the room and puts on a **blindfold.**
While It is away, the other players decide which animal they are going to be; it must be an animal that makes a noise.
The blindfolded person is led into the room and must find a lap to sit on. Nobody must help.
The person whose lap It has sat on must make a noise like the animal that was chosen.

The player who is It must then guess two things: the name of the animal, and the name of the person whose lap he or she is sitting on.
If It guesses correctly, he or she can sit down and join the other players. The person on whose lap It has been sitting then becomes It.
If It guesses incorrectly, he or she must find another lap and try again.
When a new person becomes It all the players must change places and choose another animal before starting again.

Stepping stones

All the players line up in pairs behind a starting line. A finishing line should be marked about 11 yards away. Each pair needs **two pieces of cardboard** about 20 inches square. At the word "Go!" one player of each pair throws down one of the cardboards. The other player jumps on it with both feet. The first player then places the second cardboard in front of his or her partner. While the partner is jumping, the first player runs back, picks up the cardboard which has been left behind and again puts it in front of the jumping partner. The race continues until one pair crosses the finishing line. At this point, the players change places and race back. If the jumper's foot touches the ground, both players must return to the starting line.

Transportation souvenirs

There are all kinds of things connected with transportation which you can collect. Save the **tickets** from your trips and ask other people to save theirs for you. You might get different tickets for animals, children and bicycles as well as the regular ones. Bus and railroad companies issue free **pamphlets** describing interesting places and how to get there. Ask in travel agents' for **posters** and **stickers**. When you go on trips, buy postcards of the train, boat, plane or ferry you traveled on. Use your collection to make a collage. Show your route on a map by sticking each item on with **glue.**

Footprints

You might think that all feet look the same, but if you become a footprint collector, you'll be amazed to find how different they are. Persuade your family and friends to put their feet into a **tray of poster paint.** Or you can paint the bottoms of their feet with a **paintbrush.** Then press them on **paper.** Let the prints dry. Then tie the papers all together with **string** to make a book. Another idea would be to stick all the prints on a large sheet of paper with **glue,** and ask everyone to sign his or her own footprint.

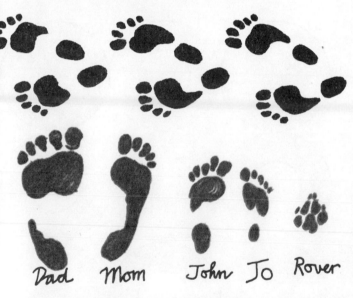

Dad   Mom   John   Jo   Rover

If you can't collect footprints in paint, look for footprints made in damp soil outside by different humans, animals and birds. Project 6 explains how you can take a plaster cast of a footprint.

Mobile tins

Tins and cans are usually thrown away after their contents have been used. But old tins can often be found in basements, gardens sheds and junk shops. Collect decorative modern tins, too, after the candy, tobacco, tea or shoe polish inside them has been used up.

Make a mobile with your most colorful **tins.**
1. Ask an adult to help you punch a hole in the center of each tin lid, using a **hammer** and **nail.**

1

Using **scissors,** cut a length of **string** for each of your tins. Pull the string through the hole in the lid. Make a knot in the end of the string on the inside of the lid.
2. If it is a soft drink can, pull the string through the other hole to knot it, as shown.

2

3. Tie the other end of each of the pieces of string to a **coat hanger** and hang up the mobile.

3

Mystery line

Use a **pencil** and **ruler** to draw a rectangle $5\frac{1}{2}$ inches by 3 inches on a sheet of paper (or carefully trace the diagram). Draw in a diagonal line as shown. Now, starting $\frac{1}{2}$ inch in from the left-hand edge, rule ten lines $\frac{1}{2}$ inch apart across the rectangle. All the lines must stop $\frac{1}{4}$ inch from the top and bottom edges of the rectangle.
Cut out the rectangle with **scissors.**
Then cut along the dotted diagonal line so that you have two triangles.

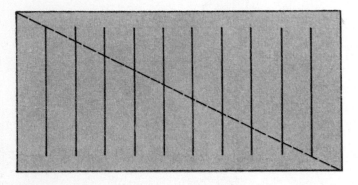

Slide the two triangles together as shown in the diagram below.
You'll see that there are now only nine lines going across the rectangle.
Can you explain what has happened to the tenth line which you drew?

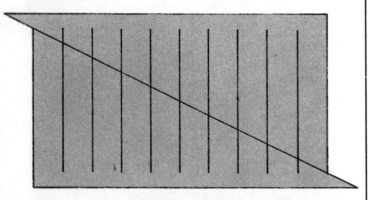

(The explanation is given on the Answers pages in the back of the book.)

Row upon row

To do this puzzle, find **six coins or counters of one type or color and six more of a different type.**
Arrange the coins or counters in rows as shown.
Now, by touching only one coin or counter, rearrange the rows so that each one consists of three identical coins or counters.
A clue: to rearrange the rows correctly, you need to make two movements with the chosen coin or counter.

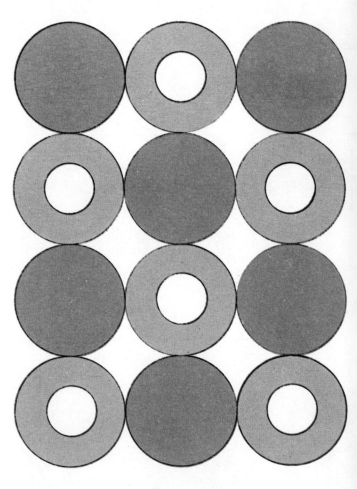

(The solution to this puzzle is given in the back of the book.)

Sporting chance

There are 14 sports and games illustrated here. Can you help the little girl find them?

The big fight

Which is the bigger of the two giants who are about to fight each other?
(Check your answer by measuring both men with a **ruler.**)

Paper lanterns

Lanterns make pretty decorations for parties all
year around. Here's how to make the pink one.
With a **pencil** and **ruler**, draw a rectangle 6½
inches by 6 inches on **pink paper.** Cut it out with
scissors. Fold the paper in half lengthwise. Make
straight cuts across the paper all along the fold,
about ¼ inch apart. Don't cut right across the
paper, but leave a border about ½ inch deep.
Open the paper out.

Draw and cut out a rectangle of **green paper**
7 inches by 4¼ inches. Curve this paper into a
long tube and stick the edges together with **glue.**
Spread glue along the long edges of the pink
paper, on the inside. Fold it around the green
tube so that it fits neatly. Cut a thin strip of
paper to make a handle and glue it into place.
Make more lanterns in other colors. Fold them
in different places to change the shapes.

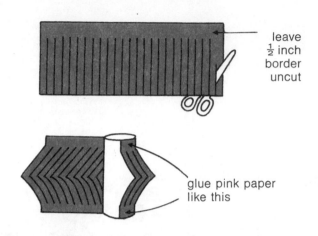

leave
½ inch
border
uncut

glue pink paper
like this

Curly picture

Most pictures on paper are *two-dimensional* (or flat). Here's a *three-dimensional* paper picture (it has depth). Paint the inside of a **cardboard box lid** using **poster paint** and a **paintbrush.**
With **scissors,** cut thin strips of **colored paper** narrower than the depth of the lid. Arrange some paper strips edge down inside the lid to make a face.

Pull some strips of paper firmly against the side of the scissors so that they curl.
Pour some **glue** into an **old dish.** Dip one edge of the paper strips into the glue and replace them in the lid to make a face. Arrange the curly strips on edge to make hair. Add more strips to make jewelry, a mustache or a bow. Let the strips dry.

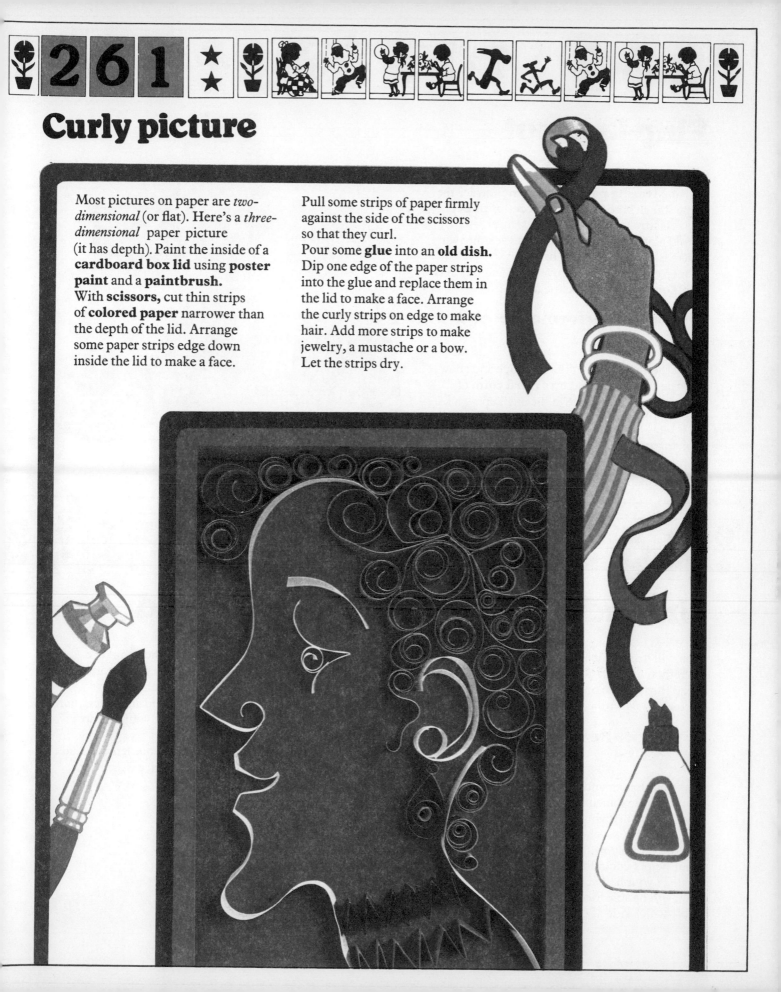

262 ★★

Flap jackpot

Here's a way to double your money!
1. Using **tracing paper** and a **pencil,** trace the shape shown here on to **two pieces of paper.** Use **scissors** to cut out the two shapes.
2. Fold along the dotted lines and stick the two papers back to back with **glue.**
3. Open one side of the "envelope" and put in **two small coins.** Then close the flaps.

★★★★ Performance ★★★★

Open the empty side of the envelope and show it to the audience. Hold up a **third coin,** of the same type as the two in the envelope. Put this third coin in the envelope, and then close the flaps.
Say some magic words and turn around once as you secretly turn over your envelope.
Open the flaps and show your audience two coins!

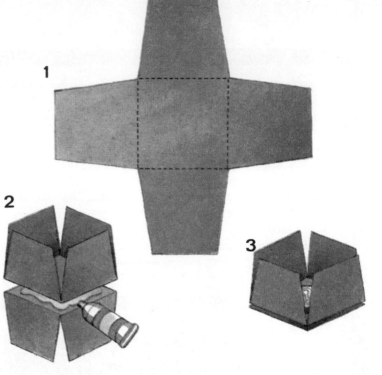

1

2

3

---

263 ★

Underdog

You will need a friend to cooperate with you secretly for this trick.
Read through the project, then work out some secret signals with your friend.

★★★★ Performance ★★★★

Ask your helper and some friends to sit at a table. While someone spins a **coin,** crawl under the table so that you cannot see what is happening. The friend who is helping sends you a secret signal. If the coin shows "heads," for instance, your helper could lift his or her right foot. For "tails," your helper could lift his or her left foot. You will be able to tell your friends at the table which side of the coin is showing.

---

264 ★

Holey hand

An *optical illusion* happens when your eye deceives your brain. This one will surprise you. Roll a sheet of **paper** into a tube.
Hold the tube in your left hand and place your right hand flat against it, with your thumb hooked lightly underneath.
Look through the tube with your left eye, and at your hand with your right eye. Keep both eyes open. You will see a hole in your hand!

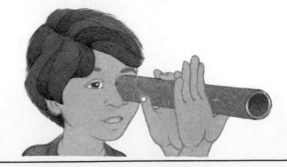

Hanky-panky

Practice this trick to be perfect.
Tie one end of a piece of **thread** to a **candy with a wrapper.**
With a **needle,** sew the other end of the thread halfway along one edge of a **handkerchief.**

★★★★ Performance ★★★★

1. Hold the handkerchief by the two corners of the edge to which the candy is attached. It hangs down behind and cannot be seen.
2. Fold the hanky in half, hiding the candy.
3. Tip the folded hanky so that the candy appears to roll out and drop into a **box.**
Lift the hanky so the candy is hidden again.
Repeat the three steps several times. Everyone will think the box is full of candy.
4. Tip up the box and show that it is empty.

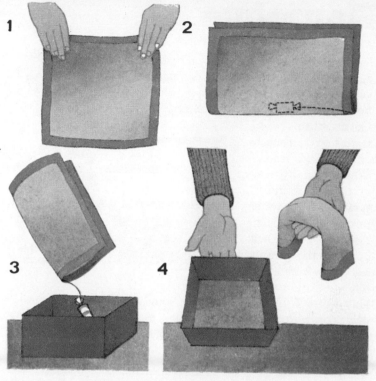

Fruit salad

How you make an orange turn into an apple will really baffle your audience.
Cut the skin of an **orange** neatly into two or three segments with a **knife.** Scoop out the fruit with a **spoon.** (Save it to eat later.)
Put an **apple** inside the orange peel and close it up so that the orange looks quite whole.

★★★★ Performance ★★★★

Cover the orange with a **handkerchief.**
Pull the handkerchief away, making sure that you pull the orange peel with it.
Show your audience an apple!

Magnetic finger

Make believe you have a magnetic finger.
Hold a **matchstick** between your middle finger and your forefinger, so that it cannot be seen.
Put your fingertip on the top of a **salt shaker.**
1. Without letting anyone see, push the matchstick into the hole at the top of the salt shaker.
2. Lift your hand up. It will look as if the salt shaker is sticking to it.

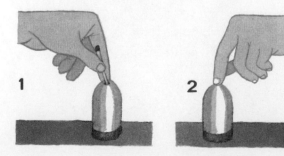

Aquarium

You can raise fish at home if you make your own aquarium. The best tanks are rectangular, but you can see different types at a pet shop. (Do not use fish bowls; they are too small.)

Collect **sand** from a river, a beach or a builder's yard. Wash it well by rinsing it in a **bucket** and pouring off the water until it is quite clean. **Ask an adult** to help you with this project.

1. Place a 2 inch layer of sand on the bottom of your **tank. Water plants** can be bought or collected from a nearby pond. They, too, must be washed. Press the plant roots into the sand. Then anchor them until they are firmly rooted.

2. To do this, tie a **small stone** to each of the plants with **thread.** Wait a week before putting in the **fish.** Goldfish, guppies, sticklebacks and mollies are all suitable fish for an aquarium. Buy them from a pet shop. Don't mix unsuitable fish, such as goldfish and sticklebacks, which sometimes fight and may even kill one another. Check that the fish you buy do not have fungus (it looks like absorbent cotton), drooping fins or dull eyes. Put a few **water snails** in with the fish. They are good *scavengers* (creatures that consume waste matter) and keep the water clean. Feed your fish with **worms, water fleas** or **commercial fish foods.** Do not give them bread. Above all, don't overfeed your fish – you could kill them with kindness!

269 ★★

Memory map

How well do you know the area around your home? Sit down with a **pencil** and **paper,** and draw from memory a plan of your route from home to school. Draw in the houses, shops, churches, gas stations and trees, as well as the streets.

Mark in gardens, bridges, rivers and sports arenas. Also mark fishing spots and places where you've seen animals or birds. Use special symbols for all these things. Draw symbols, too, for the places where you go when it rains and when the sun shines.

Ask an adult for a **street map** of the area, and compare your map with it. How much did you remember? Add to your map as you notice more.

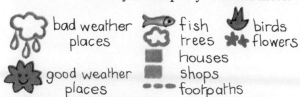

bad weather places
good weather places
fish
trees
houses
shops
footpaths
birds
flowers

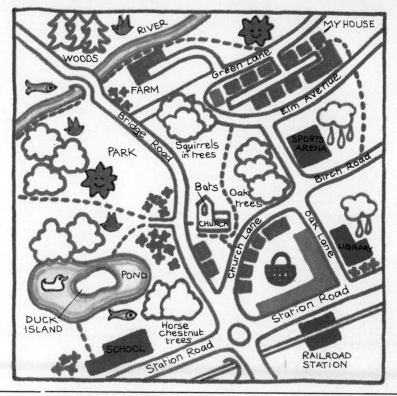

270 ★

Eggshell garden

Save the eggshells from your breakfast and turn them into mustard and watercress for your dinner salad! Push two halves of an **eggshell** inside one another so that you have an extra-strong shell. Repeat this with **half a dozen empty eggs.** Stick two pieces of **thread** 10 inches long to the base of each eggshell with **cellophane tape.** Draw the four ends of the thread above the shell and stick them in place on four sides so that they hold the shell securely. Knot the four threads together at the top.

Put a **spreading branch** in a **flowerpot** full of **soil.** Hang the eggshells from the twigs. Put some soil into each shell, and plant **mustard and watercress seeds** in them. Put the shells in a sunny place, keep them watered and wait!

Friction race

Friction is caused by one surface rubbing on another. Play this game on different kinds of paper to see the different effects of friction.

Use **cellophane tape** to bind **two coins** together.
Tape one end of a long piece of **thread**
to the two coins.
Fix the other end to a **third coin.**
(Each player needs a coin weight like this.)

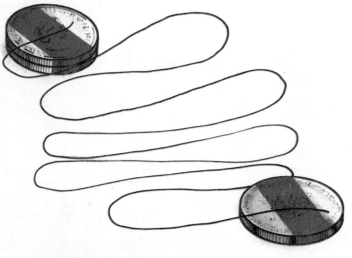

Make one racetrack from **ordinary paper** and another one from **paper with a raised surface.**
With a **ruler** and **pencil**, measure and mark spaces 1¼ inches apart across each sheet of paper.
Use **felt-tipped pens or crayons** to shade each space (or track) a different color.
With **masking tape,** fix the papers so that the tracks end on the edge of a **table.**
Play on the smooth sheet of paper first, and then on the rough one.
Each player chooses one racetrack and holds his or her coin weight on it so that the single coin hangs over the edge of the table.
At the word "Go!" the coins are released, and the first one over the edge wins.

The coins move more quickly on the smooth paper because rough surfaces produce more friction, and this holds the coins back. Also, as the coins pick up speed, the friction between them and the paper surface decreases, so they move even more quickly near the edge of the table.

White light

You'd be surprised to find out how many colors make up pure white or white daylight. Make this spinner to find out.

trace pattern

With a **pencil** and **tracing paper,** copy the big circle onto **stiff cardboard.** Mark the divisions with a **ruler.** Use **scissors** to cut out the circle.

1

1. Paint each part with **poster paints** in the colors shown. With a **needle,** make two holes as marked on the trace pattern.

2. Thread a piece of **strong thread** about 20 inches long through the holes and knot the ends of the thread together.

2

3. Holding each end of the loop, turn the cardboard around and around until the thread is tightly twisted, as shown.

3

4. Pull gently on the loops, and the cardboard will spin. Watch the colors on your cardboard merge into white as the cardboard spins faster and faster.

4

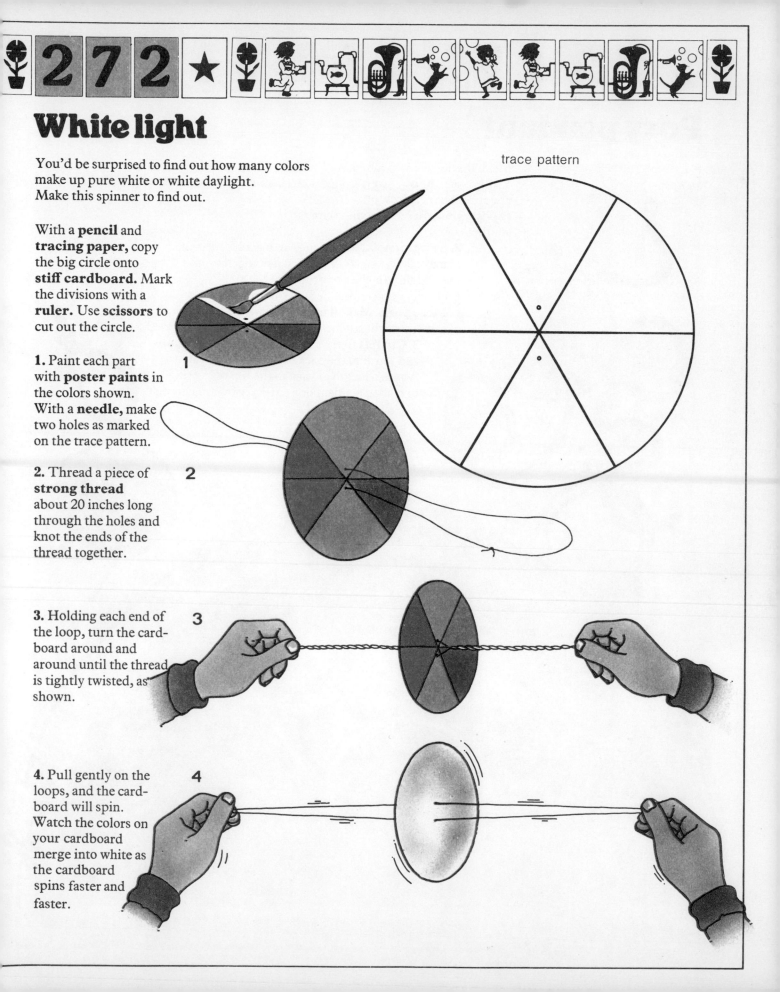

Posy pendant

Make this attractive pendant for a friend.

1. Bind some **heavy yarn** around a **curtain ring** about 2½ inches across, until it is covered. Using a **tapestry needle,** sew around the edge in another color.

2. Sew **green yarn** back and forth across the ring to make flower stalks. Tie the stalks together in the middle to make a bunch.
Embroider flowers on the stalks in **brightly-colored yarn.** Make daisy shapes with a circle of short, straight stitches.

3. Cut **felt** to the size of the ring with **scissors** and sew it to the back to hide the knots.
Attach a length of yarn to the top of the ring to make a pendant or a **safety pin** for a brooch.

Piggy bank

This money box will really brighten up your room – and keep your money safe!
With a **rolling pin,** roll out several lumps of **self-hardening clay** between two pieces of **old cloth.**
Blow up a **balloon** and tie it. Mold the clay all around the balloon, except for the neck. Leave a hole big enough to get your money out again! Model ears, legs and tail and fix them to the body. Roll out and cut a rectangle of clay for the snout and fix it on as shown.
With a **knife,** carefully cut a slit in the pig's back for a money slot – but don't burst the balloon yet. When the clay is dry, pop the balloon with a **pin** and pull it out.
Paint the pig with **acrylic paints.**

Memory snap

This game will make your family concentrate so hard that – for once – they might even be quiet! Spread out a **deck of cards,** face down, on the floor or a table. The first player turns over any two cards. If they form a pair – for example, two sevens or two aces – the player removes them and takes another turn.

If they do not form a pair, they must be turned face down again and the next player takes a turn. All the other players should watch closely and try to remember which cards are where. When there are no cards left on the table, the players count up their cards. The one with the most pairs is the winner.

Hunt the word

Play this game at a party, or if it rains. Use a **felt-tipped pen** to write the letters of the alphabet onto 30 or 40 slips of **paper.** Make sure that you have more than one slip for each of the more common letters, such as "s," "t," "a," "e," and "h."
One player is chosen to be the "wordmaker." He or she thinks of a word, but tells the other players only what subject it comes from – such as animal names or food. All the players leave the room while the wordmaker hides the letters which make up the word in different places. The other players come back and hunt for the letters. When they find one, they must not pick it up or mention it to another player. When someone guesses the word that the wordmaker thought of, all the slips are collected, and the winner becomes the wordmaker.

Place the pebble

Find some friends who are about the same height as yourself for this game.

Draw a line with a piece of **chalk** to make a starting line, or use a piece of **string** if you are indoors. Taking turns, each player should stand behind the starting line with a **pebble** in his or her hand. The player must then try to place the pebbles as far as possible away from the starting line. The player's feet must not go over the line, and no part of his body must touch the ground, except one hand which can be used for support. If he or she slips, or allows any part of the body apart from the support hand to touch the ground over the line, that player is out.

The player who places the pebble the furthest away from the starting line is the winner.

Hundreds

This is an outdoor game for two players. Using a **stick or** an **old spoon,** dig a shallow hole in a suitable place outside. If you are playing on concrete, you can use **chalk** to draw a small circle instead. Make a starting line with chalk or **string** about 3 yards away. The players take turns to shoot at the hole or circle with **marbles.** For each shot which lands on target, the player receives ten points. For each shot which misses the target, he or she loses ten points.

The first player to score 100 is the winner.

Leaf calendar

There are so many lovely varieties of leaves to collect, and most of them change throughout the year. Any park, garden or forest will give you a good start for your collection. Press your **leaves** in the same way that you press flowers. (See Project 134.) Or lay your leaves one at a time between two pieces of **blotting paper** and **ask an adult** if you can use a warm **iron** to press them until they are flat and dry. Use your leaves to make greeting cards or to decorate a box, tray or lampshade. Or keep them in a scrapbook and label each one.

Another way to display your leaves is to make a leaf calendar. For this, you need to collect **leaves** from the same tree over a whole year. Using a **ruler** and **pencil**, divide a piece of **cardboard or paper** into quarters. Print the names of the four seasons in large letters at the top of each section with a **felt-tipped pen.** In each square, draw or paint a tree without its leaves. Now find a tree with interesting leaves and collect samples. Press and dry them, then stick them down on the appropriate section of your calendar with **glue.**
In every season after that, return to the same tree and collect another batch of leaves to add to your calendar.
Or you can collect leaves from different kinds of trees, such as oak, ash and elm. Then glue them to your tree calendar as each season comes along.

Decorations

Think of all the tinsel fairies, toy rabbits and white bells that are used to decorate Christmas trees, Easter cakes and wedding tables! Why not save the ones that other people don't want? This is an inexpensive hobby, and one that can be interesting, too.

Ask your librarian for a book that explains why eggs are associated with Easter, or why guests throw rice at weddings.

Make special settings for your **decorations** in a **large candy box.** From **felt,** make a spring background for an Easter collection, or a winter scene for Christmas cake decorations. Or scatter rice in your box, then arrange the toy bridal couple, sprigs of orange blossom and white bells in it.

Yarn parabola

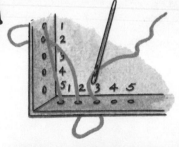

Ask people you know for leftover pieces of yarn, and you will find there is a surprising variety.

You can incorporate your **samples of different yarns** into a picture and practice geometry as well!

Find a **shallow box or box lid** and divide the four sides into equal sections about ¾ inch apart. Measure the sections with a **ruler,** then number them with a **pencil** in the order shown in the diagram.

Using a **knitting needle or darning needle,** make holes where you have marked the divisions.

Paint the box with **poster paints.** Thread a darning needle with yarn, and sew one corner of the box, as shown, from figure 1 to figure 1, figure 2 to figure 2, and so on. Repeat until all four corners are finished. In this way, you will make four *parabolas* (curves whose sides never close in a circle).

With a **felt-tipped pen,** draw the outline of a picture in the center of the box. Stick different types and colors of yarn along this outline with **white glue.** Fill in the outline with more yarn until the picture is complete.

Upside down

Whatever is happening to this boy ? Look at the picture upside down and you might change you opinion.

Extending square

This puzzle might seem difficult at first, but there is a simple, though ingenious, solution. Using **scissors,** cut out a piece of **paper** this size. Now cut it so that it will touch both sides of a **door frame** at the same time. The paper must remain in one piece. (Find out how to do it by looking in the back of the book.)

Search the studio

This artist's studio is in a mess. Can you help him find 20 tubes of paint?

Jigsaw jumble

It is easy and cheap to make your own jigsaw puzzles. Try it by cutting up **old postcards or magazine pictures** which you have first pasted onto **cardboard** with **glue.** Use **scissors** to cut your picture into sections, as shown in either diagram.

When you have done a puzzle a few times, you can make it more difficult by mixing two puzzles together and trying to sort them out as well as putting them together. Keep each puzzle in a separate **envelope** so the pieces don't get lost or mixed up.

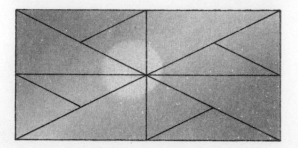

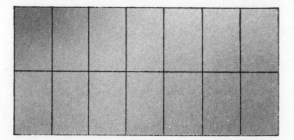

Insect eaters

Insect-eating plants are fascinating to watch – and you won't need a flyswatter in the house!
Ask for these plants at a local garden center. Some which are easy to keep are the Venus Fly Trap, the Yellow Trumpet Plant, Huntsman's Cap, Sundew and Pitcher Plant.
If you buy your plant as a bulb, put it in a **pot** in **rich, peaty soil.** Stand it in a **saucer** of **water** to keep it moist all the time. Cover the pot with a **glass jar** or a **plastic bag** held in place by a **rubber band.** Remove the cover as soon as leaves have formed. Keep the plant in a warm, sunny spot.
Feed your insect eater with **flies, wasps** and other **insects** or with pieces of **meat, cheese** and **egg white.** Insect-eating plants attract insects to them, so your plant should be able to catch some of its meals without your help!

Perfumery

Make fragrant gifts in the summer to give to friends and relatives.
Ask an adult if you can collect the **petals** from some newly-blooming, scented flowers. If you want a really definite perfume, make sure that the flowers are similarly scented.
Pack the petals into a **jar** as tightly as you can. Fill the jar with **water** and screw the **lid** on firmly to keep out any air.
Leave the jar in a cool place for at least a month. Keep adding water if necessary.
When the month is up, use a **fine-meshed sieve** to strain the liquid from the petals.
Pour the liquid into **tiny bottles** and tie a **colored ribbon** around each one.

Seascape

Shells that you have collected on vacation can
be used to decorate all kinds of things.
Collect **shells, sand** and **seaweed** during your
vacation at the seashore. (Do not take shells that
have animals still living inside them.)
1. Wash and scrub the shells thoroughly, using
an old **nail brush.**

1

2. To make a decorative jar, coat a plain **pot
or jar** with **white glue.** Cover it with sand. Shake
off the loose sand when the glue is dry.

2

Glue on shells and dried seaweed pods in waves
and bands around the outside of the pot. Decorate
boxes, mirrors and picture frames in the same way.

Chocolate petals

Make these delicious, summery treats from rose
petals, to eat or use as cake decorations.
Ask an adult if you can use the stove.

1

1. Melt some **chocolate** in a **double boiler**
(the bottom part *must* have water in it).
Or use two saucepans, one on top of the other.
Use very low heat.

2

2. Collect some fresh **rose petals** and cover one
side with melted chocolate. Put the rose petals
onto a sheet of **waxed paper,** chocolate side
up. Remove carefully when they are dry.

Tube tease

Make things vanish and reappear mysteriously! With **scissors,** cut out three pieces of **thin cardboard,** 12 inches by 12 inches, 12 inches by 10 inches and 12 inches by 8 inches. Bend the cardboard to make three tubes.

1. Fix the tube seams with **cellophane tape.** Decorate the outside of the two larger tubes with **poster paints or crayons.** Fit the three tubes inside one another.

2. Put a **colored scarf** and some **ribbons** inside the smallest tube. Make sure that they cannot be seen by your audience.

★★★★ Performance ★★★★

3. Take out the second tube and show it to be empty. Put it back inside the large tube. Now pick up the large tube and show it empty. Put the large tube back over the second tube. In this way, the smallest tube is never seen by the audience.
4. Now amaze your audience by pulling out the ribbons and then the scarf.

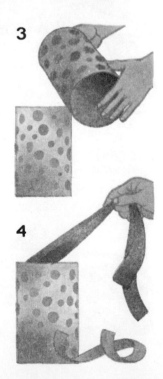

Tabletop

Practice this trick carefully before showing it. Sit at a **table** facing your audience. Put a **glass tumbler** upside-down on the table.
1. Wrap a **newspaper** around the tumbler.

2. With the right hand, move these to the edge of the table near you.

With the left hand, point at the table top.
3. At the same time, let the tumbler drop from the paper onto your lap.

Move the empty paper to the center of the table. No one knows that the tumbler is not in the paper. Crush the paper onto the table top.
Put your other hand under the table, so that it seems to be underneath the place where the paper is.
4. As you bring it back, pick up the tumbler from your lap and show it to the audience. It looks as if the tumbler went straight through the tabletop.

Under cover

Make a ribbon pass right through a matchbox!
1. Carefully undo one side of a **matchbox** cover.

1

2. Place a dab of **chewing gum** on the inside surface of the open portion of the cover.

2

Press it back against the side of the matchbox so that it looks whole again.

★★★★ Performance ★★★★

3. Thread a ribbon through the top of the matchbox cover and put the drawer back in.

3

4. Ask two friends each to hold one end of the ribbon. Cover the matchbox with a **handkerchief.**

4

Put your hands under the handkerchief, open the side of the matchbox cover and remove the ribbon.
5. Stick the box together again and take it out from beneath the handkerchief.

5

Rainbow illusion

This trick looks magical, but it is really an *optical illusion* (when the eye tricks the mind). With a **pencil** and **tracing paper,** trace this shape twice onto a piece of **thin cardboard.** Color the shapes with **felt-tipped pens** so that they look like rainbows. Cut out with **scissors.** Hold one rainbow above the other. The one on top will look smaller. Now hold the other rainbow on top. This time it will seem to be smaller – yet you know they are the same size.

Telltale fist

Good observation can sometimes make your audience think you are a mind reader!

★★★★ Performance ★★★★

Put a **coin** on a table, then turn your back on it. Ask someone to pick up the coin and hold it in the right fist against the forehead while counting up to twenty.
Ask everyone else to hold up their right fists in the same way.
Turn around to face the audience. Look at everyone's fists. The person with the whitest hand is the one who took the coin.

Pencil holder

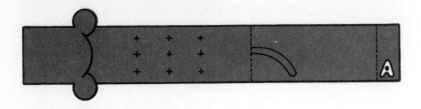

This helpful mouse will hold your pencils neat and tidy and ready for action!

Copying the diagram, draw the mouse shape in **pencil** on a sheet of **cardboard.** It should be about 12 inches by 3½ inches .

Cut out the shape with **scissors.** Cut along the solid outlines of the tail, leaving it attached to the body along the dotted line.

Make crisscross cuts in the mouse's back. This is where the pencils will go.

Fold the cardboard along the dotted lines. Let the tail stick out at the back.

Bending the cardboard shape around, press flap A beneath the mouse's nose and stick it with **glue.** Find two colored **sticky labels** for each eye and one for the nose. Peel them off the backing paper and press them in place to make the face. Glue on thin **strips of paper** for the whiskers. Push your **pencils** through the cuts in the mouse's back. Now make a pencil cat, too!

Rocking bird

This rocking bird will tip backward and forward if you give it a gentle push with your finger.

Bend an empty **soft drink or beer can** over a **ruler,** as shown.

With a **pencil,** draw the shape of the bird's head on a piece of **cardboard,** following the shape in the picture. Allow an extra semicircular flap at the bottom.

Cut out the head with **scissors.**

Draw around it and cut out a second head exactly the same.

Bend the flaps outward and stick the two head pieces (but not the flaps) together.

Spread **household cement** onto the bottom of the flaps and fix them to the bottom of the can.

When the glue is dry, paint the cardboard head and the can with **acrylic paints.**

If the bird seems top heavy and does not rock properly, push a lump of plasticine inside the hole in the base.

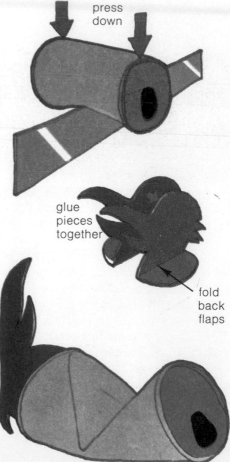

press down

glue pieces together

fold back flaps

Floating needle

If you drop a needle into water,
it will sink – but you can make
it float on the surface.

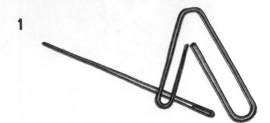

1. Bend a **paper clip,** as shown.
2. Hook a **needle** through the bent
paper clip and lower it very slowly
into a **glass of water.**
The needle will stay on the
surface of the water as you lower
the paper clip.

3. Carefully take the paper clip out
of the water, leaving the needle
floating. The needle floats
because it is supported by *surface
tension* (the surface of the water
acts like a skin which stops the
needle from sinking).

If you look in a pond, you may see
insects, such as water beetles,
which can walk across the water,
supported by surface tension.
Surface tension is normally broken
when objects are dropped heavily
into water.

Red sea

Cause a colorful, miniature explosion.
Fill a **small, open bottle** with **hot water.**
1. Pour in enough **red ink** to color the water.
Tie a piece of **string** securely around the top of
the bottle, leaving a loose end.
2. Holding the string, lower the bottle into a
large jar three-quarters full of **cold water.**
3. As it disappears under the surface, a cloud
of red water will rise out of the small bottle
and spread over the surface of the cold water.
This happens because hot water is lighter than
cold. It is lighter because the spaces between
water particles are larger in hot water. This
means that hot water will at first rise above
cold water – though they will mix together
after a short while.

Hygrometer

With this hygrometer, you can measure the humidity (dampness) in the air around you.

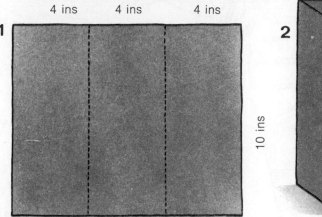

4 ins　　4 ins　　4 ins

1

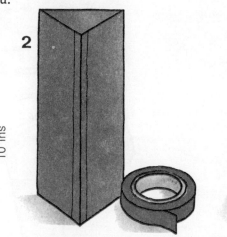

2

10 ins

3

1. Bend a piece of **cardboard** 12 inches by 4 inches in two places, as shown.
2. Join the two long edges with

cellophane tape to make a stand. Take a **long hair** from your own or a friend's head. Make a small loop at one end, and join it with tape.

3. Use a **thumbtack** to hang the loop from the top of the cardboard stand. Make sure that the hair can swing freely.

4. Use a **pencil** to draw a pointer $2\frac{1}{2}$ inches by 1 inch on **cardboard.** Cut out the shape with **scissors.** Tie the other end of the hair to the pointer about $1\frac{1}{4}$ inches from the blunt end of the pointer. Fix it with tape.
5. Press a **second thumbtack** through the blunt end of the pointer. Then push it into the stand so that the hair holds the pointer horizontal.
6. Use a **compass** to draw an arc just beyond the sharp end of the pointer. Divide the arc into ten equal sections and number them.

As the air gets drier, the hair will *contract* (get shorter) and, as the dampness in the air increases, the hair will then *expand* (get longer). This will move the pointer up and down.

4

$2\frac{1}{2}$ ins

1 inch

5

6

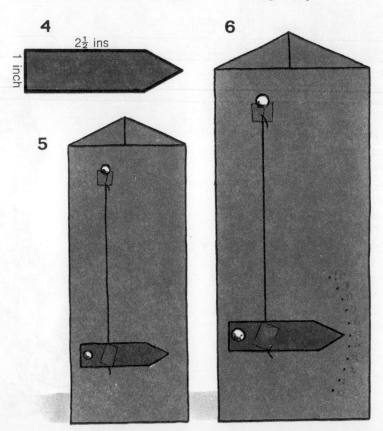

 300 ★

What's your job?

This is an outdoor game for several players. One player is chosen to be "It." He or she faces the other players, who stand about 2 yards away in a line. About 5 yards behind the players, a **place or object** – such as a tree, a stick or a line – should be chosen as "Home."

It asks one of the other players, "What do you do?" The person who has been asked must then act out any job (for example, a bricklayer, a ballet dancer or a vet).

If It guesses the job correctly, the "actor" must immediately race for Home. It must try to catch the actor before he or she gets Home. If the actor gets Home without being caught, he or she becomes It, and the game starts again.

 **301** ★

Guzzle game

This party game will make you laugh – but don't choke on the chocolate!

All the players kneel in a circle. In the center, place a **large bar of chocolate,** a **knife** and **fork** and a **set of old clothes** (for example, a dress, hat, scarf, gloves and galoshes).

The players take turns throwing a **die.**

The first player to throw a six goes into the center of the circle, puts on all the clothes as quickly as possible, and starts to eat the chocolate with the knife and fork.

The other players continue to throw the die. As soon as one gets a six, he or she runs into the center, takes the clothes off the "guzzler," puts them on, and starts to eat the chocolate. Each player who throws a six takes over until all the chocolate is eaten.

302

Play detective

Here is a shivery party game! Tear slips of **paper** for all the players. Write "burglar" and "detective" on two of them with a **pencil.** Fold the papers and give them out. The player who has the detective paper leaves the room. The burglar tells nobody that he or she is chosen to do the "robbery."

All the lights are switched off. The burglar chooses a victim by touching someone on the shoulder and whispering "You're robbed!" The victim utters blood-curdling cries and calls "Stop, thief!" The lights are switched on and the detective returns to try to find out who the burglar is.

The detective can ask each player three questions (for example, "Where were you at the time of the crime?"). Everyone must answer truthfully except the burglar. If the detective guesses who the burglar is, he or she wins a prize. If not, the burglar then becomes the detective.

303

Marble die

This is a game with **marbles** for two players. One player is the "target-keeper" and the other is the "shooter." The shooter starts with 5 marbles. The target is a **marble** with a **small die** balanced on top of it.
The shooter plays from a shooting line about 3 yards away from the target. If the shooter succeeds in knocking the die off the marble, he or she receives from the target-keeper the same number of marbles as the die shows when it falls. Each time the shooter misses, the shooting marble is kept by the target-keeper.
This game can be played in another way with both players as shooters. In this case, they each have a certain number of turns (say, five). The player with the highest number of marbles at the end is the winner.

Balancing act

Can you tell which of the three knitting needles will really balance on the table edge? (You will find the answer in the back of the book.)

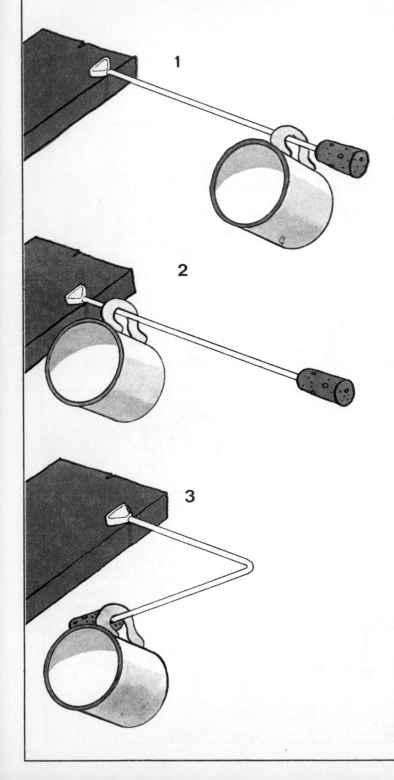

1

2

3

Spot the stranger

One of the characters in this drawing doesn't fit in with the rest. Can you spot the odd one out? (The solution is given in the Answers pages.)

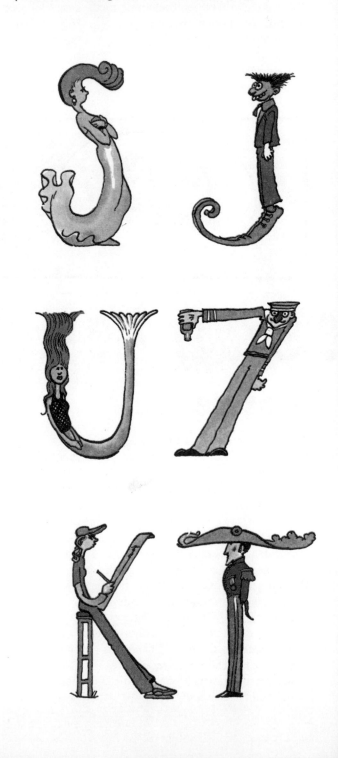

Catch a cat

It's difficult to tell what is happening here!
Can you put the events in the right order ? (The
answer is given in the back of the book.)

Which country?

These costumes come from six different countries.
Can you name them all ? (The countries are listed
in the Answers pages in the back of the book.)

Flowery eggs

Here's a way to make beautiful, decorated eggs.
Press some **flower petals** (Project 134).
Blow some **eggs** (Project 50). Coat the undersides
of the petals with **glue.** Use a pair of **tweezers**
to arrange the petals on the eggs. When dry,
paint on **polyurethane varnish** with a **brush.**

Pebble mouse

With a **pencil,** trace these ear shapes onto **paper.**
Cut them out with **scissors.** Place them on a
scrap of **leather** and cut around them. Cut a long
strip for the tail. With **household cement,** stick
the ears and tail in place on a **round pebble.**
Paint on eyes with **poster paints** and a **brush.**
Cut and glue a few **bristles** from a broom to make
whiskers!

Bottle garden

Ivies, African violets and ferns all grow
well in bottle gardens. Buy **small plants,
charcoal** and **potting soil** at a garden
shop or center.
Your friends will ask how your plants got inside!

Find a **large glass
bottle** and clean it
out well.
1. Use a **sheet of
rolled-up newspaper**
to funnel a 2 inch layer
of charcoal into the
bottle. Charcoal is
good for drainage and
helps to stop fungi
from growing.

1

Autumn glow

Decorate candles for winter with autumn leaves. Press some **autumn leaves** or make leaf skeletons (Project 210). **Ask an adult** to help you melt some **wax** in an **old double boiler.** Fix some leaves to a **candle** with **pins.** With a **brush,** paint wax thinly over the leaves. Remove the pins.

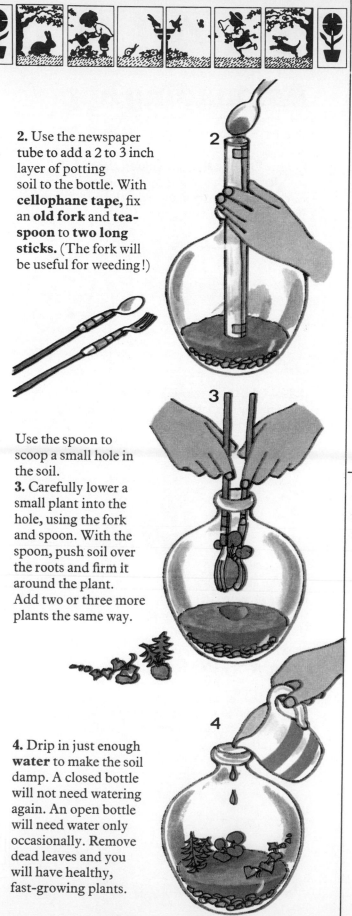

2. Use the newspaper tube to add a 2 to 3 inch layer of potting soil to the bottle. With **cellophane tape,** fix an **old fork** and **tea-spoon** to **two long sticks.** (The fork will be useful for weeding!)

Use the spoon to scoop a small hole in the soil.
3. Carefully lower a small plant into the hole, using the fork and spoon. With the spoon, push soil over the roots and firm it around the plant. Add two or three more plants the same way.

4. Drip in just enough **water** to make the soil damp. A closed bottle will not need watering again. An open bottle will need water only occasionally. Remove dead leaves and you will have healthy, fast-growing plants.

Paperweight

Transform any large, smooth **stones** which you find into decorated paperweights.
Make sure the stone is clean and dry. Choose some attractive **small shells** and **seeds,** and stick them onto the stone with **household cement.** It is a good idea to work out a pattern on a flat surface before your start gluing.
You could also paint pictures or patterns onto your stones with **poster paints.** When the colors are dry, give the stones a gloss by painting on **polyurethane varnish** with a **brush.**

Lost lollipop

This trick works best if you practice it first. With **scissors,** cut four disks out of **cardboard.** Use **poster paints** and a **brush** to color one disk red, one blue, one green and one yellow. Place a **drinking straw** between the red and green disks, and stick them together with **glue.**
1. Glue the blue and yellow disks together over the other end of the straw. Put it in a **paper bag.**

1

★★★★ Performance ★★★★

2. Take the "lollipop" from the bag to show the red side. Hide the other end in your hand.

2

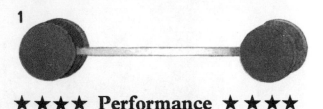

Put the lollipop back in the bag, twisting it around as you do so. Take it out and show your audience a green lollipop. Then put it back.

3

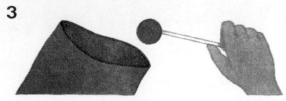

3. Take it out two more times to show first the blue and then the yellow lollipops. Always make sure the other end is hidden in your hand.
4. Take out the lollipop with the red side showing and drop it in a **box.** Show the empty paper bag. The other lollipops have vanished!

4

Astounding apple

Hand a friend a whole apple – which has already been sliced!
1. Thread a **needle** with **strong thread** and push it under the skin of a soft **apple.** Sew with long stitches under the skin until the thread has gone all the way around the apple.

1

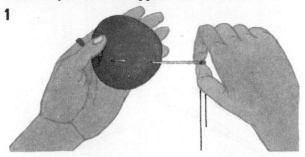

2. Hold the two ends of the thread and pull them firmly so that the thread slices through the soft part of the apple.

2

Sew the apple in another direction to slice it again. In this way, you can divide the apple into as many pieces as you like without cutting the rind.

★★★★ Performance ★★★★

Ask a friend to peel the apple with a **knife.** Watch your friend's surprise when the apple falls to pieces!

Egg-straordinary!

This trick will make your audience think you have a magic egg! Project 116 explains how it works.
Pour some **water** into **two glasses.**
1. Pour three or four tablespoons of **salt** into one of the glasses of water, and stir with a **spoon** until all the salt has dissolved.

1

★★★★ Performance ★★★★

Hand someone the glass of unsalted water and an **egg.** Tell the person to put the egg into the glass of water. The egg will sink to the bottom.
2. Take **another egg** and put it into the glass of salted water yourself. Watch your friend's surprise when your egg floats!

2

Seek the six

Baffle your friends with this trick.
Find the six of hearts from an **old deck of cards.** Cut off the left-hand edge with **scissors.**
1. With **glue,** stick this edge to the face of the three of spades, as shown.

1

Find the joker and the three of clubs.
2. Put the joker behind the three of clubs and hold them together so they look like one card.

2

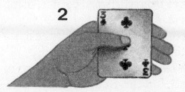

3. Put the special card behind the two cards. It now looks as if you are holding the three of spades, the six of hearts and the three of clubs.

3

★★★★ Performance ★★★★

Show the cards as in step 3.
Turn the cards over. Then spread them out between your fingers.
Ask someone to take out the six of hearts.
4. Your friend will take out the middle card – and find it is the joker!

4

Pinwheel

You can buy spinning pinwheels – but it's cheaper and more fun to make them yourself.

With **scissors,** cut out a piece of **stiff paper** for a pinwheel, about 6 inches square. Draw two diagonal lines from corner to corner, using a **ruler** and **pencil.**

1. Make cuts about 3½ inches long from each corner toward the middle of the square.

2. Using tiny dabs of **glue,** stick A to a, B to b, C to c and D to d. Let the glue dry.

Cut a piece of **garden wire** 6 inches long and make a small loop in one end of it.

Cut out a tiny diamond shape from **cardboard** and make a hole in the middle of it.

Thread the straight end of wire through the hole and then through the middle of the pinwheel.

3. Bend the wire in the back of the pinwheel into a figure eight, as shown. Wind the loose end of wire around a stick about 12 inches long. Make sure the sails can turn easily. Blow gently – and see your pinwheel spin!

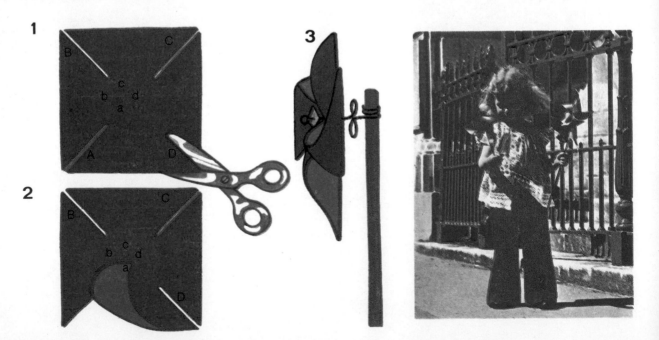

Patchwork quilt

Make a snug doll's bed out of an **empty cigar box** fitted with a miniature quilt.

With **scissors,** cut out a piece of **paper** the same size as your box. With a **pencil** and **ruler,** divide the paper into three equal strips along its width. Draw different-sized patches on them.

1. Write a letter and a number on each patch, as shown. Cut out the patch shapes.
Fix the paper patches to the wrong sides of the **scraps of cloth,** with **pins.** Cut around each patch leaving an extra ¼ inch of cloth all around.

1

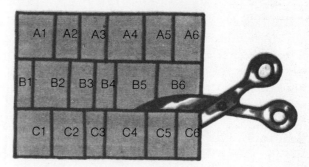

2

2. Fold the edges of cloth over and baste them down with a **needle** and **thread.**
Lay the pieces numbered A1 and A2 together, cloth sides facing each other.

3. Overcast the two long edges together, but do not sew through the paper. Sew the rest of the patches together in the same way to make the three strips. Sew the strips together.
Remove the basting stitches and the paper patches. Hem the outer edge of the quilt and line the back if you wish.

Indoor fountain

You can make a fountain for your bedroom with this experiment and find out about air pressure.

1. Ask an adult to punch two holes in the **lid of a screw-top glass jar** with a **hammer** and a **nail.** Cut 2½ inches off a **plastic straw** with **scissors.**

2. Push the straw down into one hole so that half the straw comes out the other side. Push a **whole plastic straw** down into the other hole so that it just comes out the other side. Seal the straws in place with **plasticine.**

3. Pour enough **water** into the jar to make it about one-quarter full. Screw on the lid.

4. Fill **another glass jar** with water. Color the water with drops of **colored ink.**

5. Put a **bucket** on the floor near a **table** edge. Quickly turn the jar with a lid upside down so that the short straw goes into the jar with colored ink. The long straw must be right over the bucket. Water pours down the long straw, reducing the air pressure in the water jar. Air from the ink jar rushes in, to replace the air lost from the water jar, and brings the colored ink with it. This makes your fountain work.

1

2

3

4

5

INK

Spinning egg

Give one **hard-boiled egg** and one **uncooked egg** to a friend. Ask the friend to tell them apart without breaking either egg. Then show how you do it!

1. Carefully spin each egg on its side on a flat surface.

2. Touch each spinning egg briefly with your finger and then take away your finger. The egg that stops after you touch it is hard-boiled. The egg that keeps spinning is uncooked.

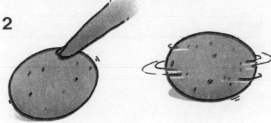

The uncooked egg keeps spinning because the inside is liquid. This liquid continues to move under its own momentum, even after you touch it, and keeps the egg spinning.

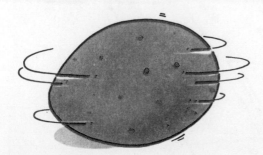

It's a gas

Carbon dioxide is the gas we breathe out, and which plants absorb during daylight. You can make this gas and see one of the things it does.

1. With **scissors,** cut a piece of **thin cardboard** big enough to cover the top of a **glass jar. Ask an adult** if you can have some **fresh bicarbonate of soda** and some **vinegar.**

2. Put a heaping **teaspoon** of the bicarbonate of soda in the glass jar. Add about $\frac{3}{4}$ inch of **water** and stir thoroughly until the powder is dissolved. Put in two or three teaspoons of vinegar, which contains acetic acid. You now have carbon dioxide. Cover the jar with the cardboard and leave until the fizzing stops.

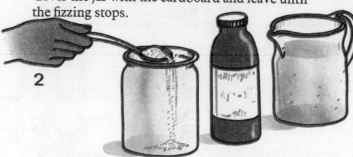

3. Ask an adult to light a **long match.** Carefully slide the cardboard off the jar. Put the burning end of the match down into the jar. The carbon dioxide will make the flame go out.

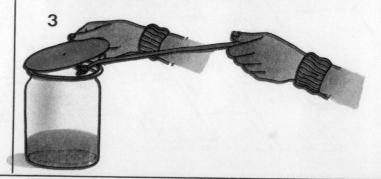

Hopscotch

There are lots of different ways to play hopscotch. Here are three patterns you can copy or you can make up your own. It is a good game to play alone or with other people.

Choose a **pavement or path** that is not being used. With **chalk,** number the paving stones, or draw the squares and then number them. Find a **stone or coin** to use as a counter.
Following pattern 1, throw the counter onto square 1. Jump over this square and land with both feet in squares 2 and 3. Hop on one foot to square 4, then jump to squares 5 and 6, and so on, until you reach 10. Here turn on one foot and come back. When you arrive at squares 2 and 3, pick up your stone and jump off.

All the players take turns to do this. On the second turn, throw the counter onto square 2 and proceed in the same way. Players must never jump into the square which their counters are occupying. If their feet or their counters land on a line or in the wrong square, those players are out and must try again for the same squares when their turns come around again. Another way of playing is to complete the course on one leg, kicking the counter from square to square as you go.

A nutty game

In autumn, wait for the beautiful, glossy **horse chestnuts** to burst out of their shells and then play this traditional game with a friend.
Ask an adult to pierce a hole through a chestnut with a **meat skewer.**
Knot one end of a piece of **string** and thread it through the chestnut. Make sure you leave a loose end of about 20 inches with which to swing the nut. Get a friend to do the same with another chestnut. The players take turns hitting their chestnut against the opponent's nut, which is held still. The object is to try to break the opponent's chestnut. The round is over when one chestnut breaks, but the winner then goes on to "fight" other chestnuts.
The winning chestnut is the one that breaks the most other nuts before being broken itself.

Nose to nose

You can't be shy when you play this party game! Divide all the players into two teams, and ask them to stand in two straight lines.
Take the covers off **two empty matchboxes.** The first player in each team puts a matchbox cover on his nose. At the word "Go!", the matchbox must be put onto the nose of the next player in the line, but without either of the players using their hands. The matchbox is passed to the third player in the same way, and so on until it reaches the end of the line.
If anyone drops the matchbox cover or uses his or her hands, the matchbox must go back to the beginning of the line and that team starts all over again. The winning team is the one whose matchbox reaches the end of the line first.

Simon rules

You need several players for this game. One player should be chosen as Simon (or you can use any other name you like).
Simon stands in front of all the other players and gives them commands. The commands can be fairly easy, but some must begin with the words "Simon says" and others not. If a command starts with these words, everyone must obey. If it doesn't, nobody should move. Players who obey a command not starting with "Simon says" or who don't obey one that does, are out. The winner is the person left after everyone else is out. That player then becomes Simon.
The game should be played fast, with commands following one another as quickly as possible.

Wood scraps

Wood scraps make great wall decorations. You might find some at home, but you could also ask at a local lumberyard for spare bits of wood. Save them up to make a collage.

Ask an adult to cut a piece of **plywood** for the backing. (It can be any size you like.)
Choose **wood scraps** for their interesting shapes, colors or grains (patterns in wood).
Use **sandpaper** to smooth the edges of the wood.
Arrange the scraps on the plywood.
Put a little **wood glue** on the back of each piece and press it onto the plywood.
Use a **cloth** to wipe off the excess glue, and let the collage dry.
If you want to hang it up, **ask an adult** to drill two holes at the back for hooks and wire.

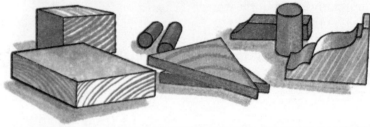

Toy menagerie

A *menagerie* is a collection of wild animals. Learn about real animals by collecting model ones. People have been doing this for over 4000 years. Today, you can buy wooden, china, stone, glass and metal models. Or you can make your own animals from felt, paper, shells, stone or model kits.
Make a cage for your animals.
Use **scissors** to cut strips of **colored cardboard** 1 inch wide and long enough to stretch across an **old shoe box.**
Fix the strips to the box with **cellophane tape** to make bars.
Decorate the cage with bright **poster paints.**

Trinkets

Trinkets are small ornamental objects. They can be buttons, buckles, beads, hatpins, lockets and so on.
Ask an adult if you may look in an old button box or sewing drawer for such things. You might find some discarded cuff links or belts with interesting fastenings.

Odd beads, barrettes and combs might turn up in jewelry boxes. Make sure you ask before you take them for your collection.

Once you have saved up a lot of trinkets, it's fun to display them in an unusual way. Make a cardboard house and decorate it with your prettiest pieces. It will look like a model for a fairy tale.

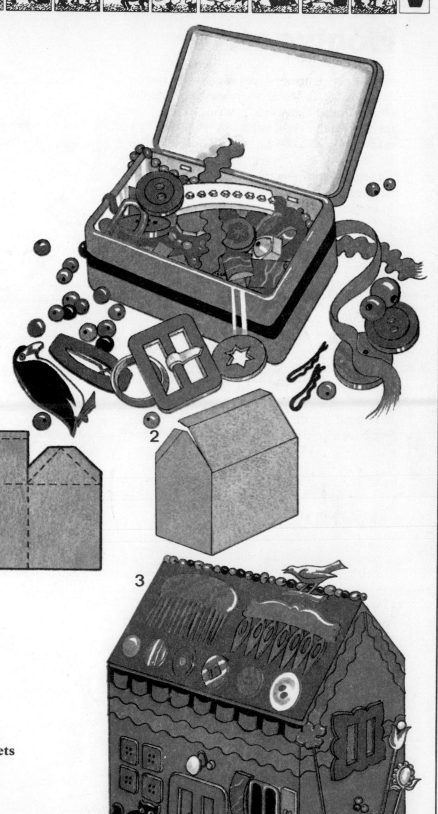

Find a piece of **stiff cardboard** 20 inches by 7 inches.

1. Use a **pencil** and a **ruler** to draw a design on it like the one shown.
Fold the cardboard along the dotted lines.

2. Use **glue** to stick the flaps together to make the shape of the house.
Paint the model with bright **poster colors.**
Let the paint dry.

3. Use **household cement** to stick your **trinkets** into position. Use big buckles for windows and doors, buttons as roof tiles, brooches and hat-pins as climbing flowers.

Möbius strip

An ordinary loop of paper has an inside and an outside edge. A *Möbius strip* is a special loop which seems to have only one side. It was invented in the 19th century by a German mathematician named August F. Möbius.

To see how puzzling the loop is, make a Möbius strip from a piece of **paper** about 12 inches by 1¼ inches.
1. Twist one end of the paper around as shown. Join the two ends with **glue or cellophane tape.**

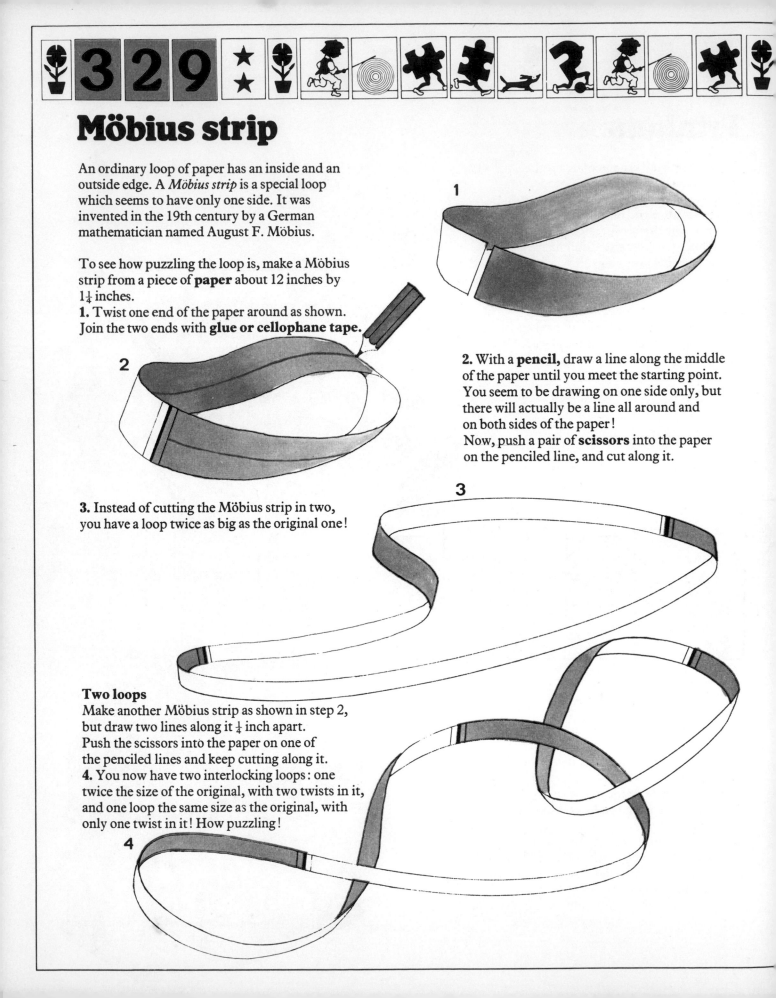

2. With a **pencil,** draw a line along the middle of the paper until you meet the starting point. You seem to be drawing on one side only, but there will actually be a line all around and on both sides of the paper!
Now, push a pair of **scissors** into the paper on the penciled line, and cut along it.

3. Instead of cutting the Möbius strip in two, you have a loop twice as big as the original one!

Two loops
Make another Möbius strip as shown in step 2, but draw two lines along it ¼ inch apart. Push the scissors into the paper on one of the penciled lines and keep cutting along it.
4. You now have two interlocking loops: one twice the size of the original, with two twists in it, and one loop the same size as the original, with only one twist in it! How puzzling!

Jolly geometry

In this diagram there are six squares (including the big one). See if you can find them all. There are also 22 triangles within the big square. Try to find them, too.

Here is another diagram. See how many squares and triangles you can find in this one. (Don't forget to count the big square itself.)
(The answers are in the back of the book.)

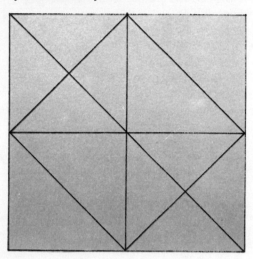

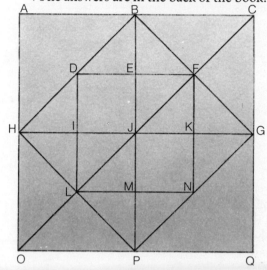

Safari sandwiches

Two hunters on safari sit down in the bush to eat their lunches. The first hunter has five sandwiches and the second one has three. As they begin to eat, a third hunter comes along. He doesn't have any sandwiches at all, so the other two offer to share their lunches with him.
The food is divided equally. After lunch, the third hunter says he will pay eight cents for the food he has eaten, but no one can agree on how to divide the money.

The first hunter says that the money should be divided in the proportion of five to three.
The second hunter says it should be divided equally, since they all ate an equal amount.
The third hunter says that the first hunter should get seven cents and the second hunter only one cent.
Can you decide who was right? (Look on the Answers pages at the back of the book to see how the money should be divided.)

Head start

To your audience, this special matchbox will look full – and then magically empty.

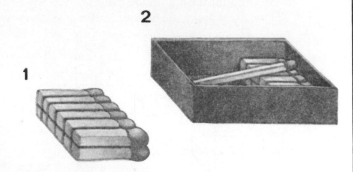

Cut several **matchsticks** in half.
1. Use **glue** to fix the head ends together.
2. Glue the head ends into one end of the **matchbox** drawer and add one **ordinary matchstick.**

★★★★ Performance ★★★★

3. Open the box to show the matchstick heads. Take out the whole matchstick. Close the box. Wave the matchstick, like a wand, over the box. At the same time, secretly turn it around.

4. Open the drawer and show it to your audience, making sure that they do not see the halved matchsticks.
The box will now appear to be empty!

Great escape

Practice this trick until you are perfect.

You will need **two small cloth bags the same color.** (Shoe bags will do.)
1. Put one bag inside the other, so that its top sticks out.
2. Hold the bags so that the top of the *inner* bag is gathered and hidden in your hand.

★★★★ Performance ★★★★

Drop a **small ball** into the *outer* bag.

3. Now, hide the top of the *outer* bag with your hand and allow the *inner* bag to stick out. Ask someone to tie the bag with **string.** (It will be the inner bag that is tied.) Ask two people to hold the ends of the string.
Put a **big scarf** over the bags.

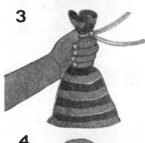

4. Using both hands, take the ball from the outer bag under the scarf.

5. Whisk away the scarf and the outer bag at the same time. Show the ball in your other hand. It seems to have escaped!

All tied up

Quick movements are needed to make two handkerchiefs seem to tie themselves together. To prepare for this trick, put a **very small rubber band** on the tip of one finger.

★★★★ **Performance** ★★★★

Show your audience **two separate handkerchiefs.** Say you can make the handkerchiefs tie themselves together in midair. Quickly slip the rubber band from your finger and around the handkerchiefs so that one corner of each is inside the rubber band. (Don't let the audience see this.) Throw the handkerchiefs up in the air. As they come down they will look as if they are tied together.

Shaky coin

Prove you can make a coin vanish by tearing up the matchbox you put it in. Prepare a special **matchbox** in secret. **Ask an adult** to cut a slit in one end of a matchbox drawer with a **knife.**

★★★★ **Performance** ★★★★

Show your audience a **coin,** and then put it in the matchbox drawer. Close the box. Hold your hand over the slit in the drawer. Shake the box until the coin comes through the slit into your hand. Show the empty matchbox. Then tear it up to prove that the coin has really vanished. (Keep the coin hidden in your hand during this part of your performance.)

Defying gravity

Have you ever heard of something rolling *up* a hill? Here's how to do it.

1

1. Use a **pencil** to draw this shape twice on a piece of **cardboard.** Cut out the shapes with **scissors.**

2

Fold the shapes around until you make cones. **2.** Fix the edges of the cones with **cellophane tape.** Tape the two cones together.

3

3. Put **two straws** against a **book** so that they are wider apart at the top than at the bottom.

4

4. Put the double cone on the straws at the bottom of the slope. It will roll uphill. (Project 362 explains why this works.)

Cardboard printing

Make a printing block to decorate your book covers, wrapping paper or greetings cards.

1. With **scissors,** cut two pieces of **stiff cardboard,** each 3 inches square.

2. Use a **pencil** to draw a simple shape on one square. Cut out the shape.

3. Use **glue** to stick the shape to the other square. Let the glue dry.

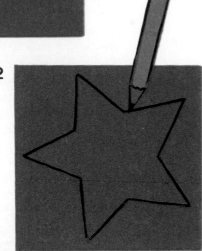

4. Paint the shape with **poster colors.**

5. Press the shape face down on **paper.** Lift off the shape. Dry it with a **tissue** and use a new color.

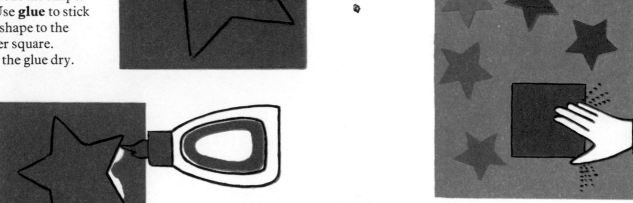

Jacob's ladder

You can make this ladder out of **cardboard or plywood.** (A wooden ladder makes a nice "clacking" sound. **Ask an adult** to cut the plywood if you want to make this kind.)

With **scissors,** cut out six pieces of **stiff cardboard,** each 2½ inches by 1¾ inches. (If an adult cuts plywood for you, make sure the corners are rounded off.)
Use **acrylic paints** and a **brush** to paint each piece a different color. Let the paint dry.

Cut 15 strips of **narrow ribbon,** each 3 inches long. With **household cement,** stick three ribbons to each piece of cardboard as shown. (Glue only ½ inch at each end of each ribbon.) Join all the pieces in the same way. Let the glue dry, then decorate the ladder by sticking on **gummed paper shapes.**

fix ribbons on like this

make sure you glue down exactly ½ inch of ribbon each time

With your thumb and forefinger, hold the top piece of cardboard by its short sides. Tip it right over, and watch the whole ladder flip. (If it doesn't work the first time, tip the top piece of cardboard the other way instead.)

Sleeping lions

Play this game with your friends at the end of a party. You may even find that some of your friends actually fall asleep while pretending to be lions! Everyone agrees on one person as the leader. The leader tells the other players that they are lions who have had a big hunt that day. While the leader counts to ten, the lions must lie down to sleep. The leader then watches to see that the lions do not move. Any lion who moves must then sit out with the leader to help spot other moving lions. The last lion left is the king of the jungle.

340 Ho hum!

Try to hum while you hold your nose and keep your mouth shut! You'll find it isn't very easy to do it for more than three seconds. See who can hum the longest of all your friends, but be careful not to hurt your ears!

341 Geography

Play this game while sitting in a circle with a group of your friends. You'll be surprised how many places you can think of!

One person begins by saying the name of a country, a town or a city. The player sitting just to the left of the first person then must name a different place that starts with the last letter of the previously-named place. For example, if "England" was the first place called, then the next player could say "Denmark." The game continues around in a circle. If someone can't think of a place that hasn't already been named, that person is out. The last player left is the winner.

Clock solitaire

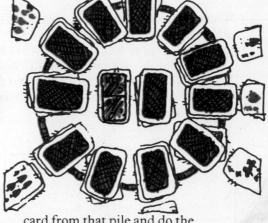

Here's a game you can play by yourself. But this doesn't mean you'll always win!

With a **pencil,** draw a clockface on a large sheet of **cardboard.** Number it as shown, except for 11 and 12. Instead of 11, draw a Jack. Instead of 12, draw a Queen. Draw a King in the center. Deal a deck of **playing cards** around the clock, face down, so that each number and face has four cards on it. Take the top card from the King pile, look at it, and put it face upward beside the pile of the same number or face. Then take the top card from that pile and do the same thing. Turn up a King card when you come to an empty space. You have won if you can put all the cards in their correct places *before* all the kings are in the center – otherwise you must start again. Good luck!

Bubbles

It's easy and quick to make a loop to blow your own bubbles – and saves you money!

Bend one end of a piece of **wire** about 10 inches long into a circle, and the other end into a small loop for a handle. Put ½ inch of **dish washing detergent** into a **yogurt container** and add one **tablespoon** of **water.**

Dip the circle into the liquid. Then raise the circle and blow gently until a bubble floats away.

Comb band

You don't have to be an accomplished musician to have your own band. All you need is a group of friends, some combs and paper.

Each player must have a **comb.** Fold a thin sheet of **tissue paper** over the teeth on a comb. Hold the paper tightly over the comb and bring it up to your mouth. Keeping your lips slightly open, "sing" as you slide the comb back and forth, so that the paper vibrates. High notes make most vibrations, but experiment with different sounds. Practice simple tunes and rounds with your friends. You could even give a concert!

Speed-up spinner

When you make this spinner it will help you understand the way gears on bicycles and cars work. The spinner is fun to play with, too!

1. With **scissors,** cut a piece of **stiff cardboard** 21 inches by 6 inches. With a **ruler** and the scissors' point, score lines on the cardboard as shown by the dotted lines.

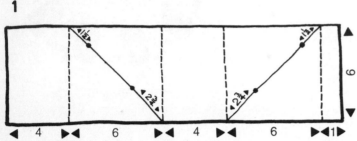

Draw two diagonal lines as shown. Use the scissors' point to make two holes 1½ inches down from the top and two holes 2¾ inches from the bottom on each diagonal line.

2. Cut out two strips of **stiff paper,** each 9¾ inches by 3 inches. Lay one on top of the other and roll into a cylinder shape. Fix the seam with **cellophane tape.** Cut cardboard circles to fit in the ends of the cylinder. Make a hole in the center of each circle just big enough to hold a pencil.
Tape one circle in each end of the cylinder. Push a **pencil** through the holes and tape it at each end so it can't be turned.

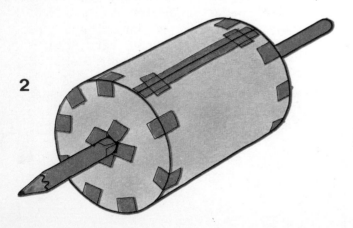

3. Pull a strong **rubber band** about 3 inches long over the cylinder. Now bend the stiff cardboard on the score lines. Push one end of the pencil into one hole 2¾ inches from the corner. Bend the cardboard around and push the other end of the pencil through the opposite hole. Tape the cardboard into a box shape.

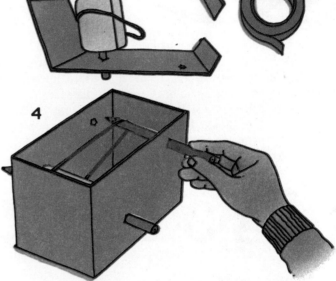

4. Push another pencil through the other two holes, hooking the rubber band over it, as shown. Draw and cut out two circles of stiff paper, 6 inches and 3 inches in diameter. Decorate them with **felt-tipped pens.** Push the small circle onto the cylinder pencil and the large circle onto the other pencil. When you turn the end of the cylinder pencil without the circle on it, the small circle will turn to make the large circle spin.

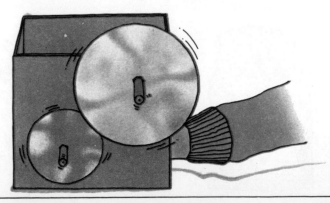

Moving sound

Make an instrument to show the vibrations, or movements, of sound.

1. Ask an adult to remove both ends of an empty **tin can** with a **can opener.** Rinse out the can with water and let it dry. If the edges of the can are sharp, cover them with **masking tape.** With **scissors,** cut a deflated **balloon** in half.

1

2. Stretch the bottom half of the balloon tightly over one end of the can. If necessary, hold the balloon in place by putting a **rubber band** around both the balloon and the can.

2

3. With **glue,** fix a small piece of **mirror** about ¼ inch square onto the outside of the stretched end of the balloon. It should be about one third of the way in from the edge of the can.

3

4. Stand opposite a **dark wall or door** (or fix a piece of **dark paper** to the wall with masking tape). Hold the can so that a shaft of daylight or light from a lamp shines onto the mirror and reflects a spot of light onto the wall. Place your mouth at the tape-covered open end of the can and make noises into it. The balloon will vibrate from the sounds you make. Both the mirror and the spot of light reflected from it onto the wall will then move according to the different sounds you make.

4

Tasty herbs

Herbs dried at home taste much better and last longer than ones bought from a store.
If you know someone who grows herbs, ask if you can pick a few sprigs from the plants. (Or buy yourself a herb plant.)

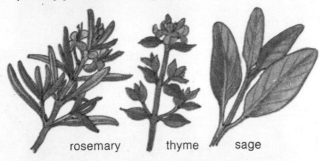

rosemary   thyme   sage

Thyme, rosemary and sage are commonly grown **herbs** which dry well. Use your dried sage or thyme in casseroles and stews, and sprinkle rosemary on lamb, fish or eggs.

Use **thread** to tie the sprigs of each kind of herb together. (Write labels for them.)
1. Hang the bunches upside down in an airy place to dry. Leave them two or three weeks.

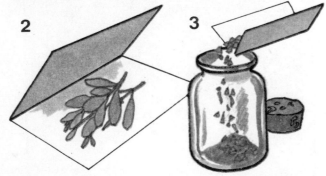

Put the dried herbs on separate sheets of **paper.**
2. Fold the paper over and rub the leaves off the stems between the doubled sheet.
3. Store dried herbs in **jars** in a cool place.

Quill pen

It is much more fun to write with this kind of pen than an ordinary ballpoint pen.
Goose feathers make the best quill pens, but you could use hen feathers instead. Ask the butcher to give you a perfect feather.
The base of the shaft (the bit that goes down the middle) should be undamaged.

Use a **kitchen knife** to scrape off the tiny fluffy bits on the shaft of the **feather.** Now **ask an adult** to help you cut and whittle the shaft on a **chopping board.**
1. Use a **penknife** to cut a slice at an angle, through the shaft to the tip.
2. Whittle the tip of the shaft into a neat point.
3. Make a cut into the tip of the pen.

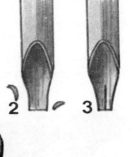

Writing
To use your quill pen, dip the point in some **ink.** Wipe off any excess ink.
Always begin to write by making a short sideways stroke on the **paper,** and then a down stroke. This gets the ink flowing.

Formicarium

A *formicarium* is a home for ants. Make one so that you can study these amazing creatures.

Buy a **wooden seed tray** about 16 inches by 12 inches from a garden center.
Line the bottom and sides of the tray with a sheet of **plastic**.
Mix up some **plaster of Paris** and **water** in an **old plastic bowl** with an **old spoon**.
1. Pour the mixture into the tray to within 1¼ inches of the top. **Ask an adult** to cut a piece of **wood** 3 inches deep and 1¼ inches shorter than the width of the seed tray.
2. Lay the wood in the wet plaster about 4 inches from one end so the top is level with the rim of the tray. Let the plaster dry.

1

2

The smaller part is the feeding area and the entrance, and the larger part is the nest.

3. Fill the larger area with **fine soil**. Use **household cement** to fix a **glass** cover over it. Cover the smaller area with a piece of removable glass.
4. Look under stones and wood in the **park or garden** for ants. You need a **queen ant** – she is the biggest ant and may have wings. Put the ants, some **honey**, and a few drops of **water** in the smaller area.
Keep **black cardboard** over the nest unless you are observing it.
Remember to give water as well as food to the ants.

3

4

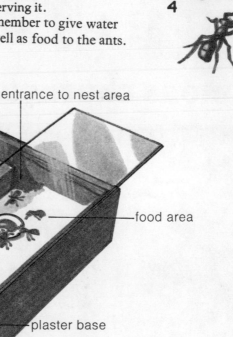

entrance to nest area

food area

plaster base

Clowning around

You may think that these two clowns are identical. But, if you look carefully, you will see that there are ten differences between them. Can you see them all?

Famous characters

These silhouettes illustrate famous characters from three well-known stories. Do you know their names?
(You will find the answers in the back of the book.)

One way out

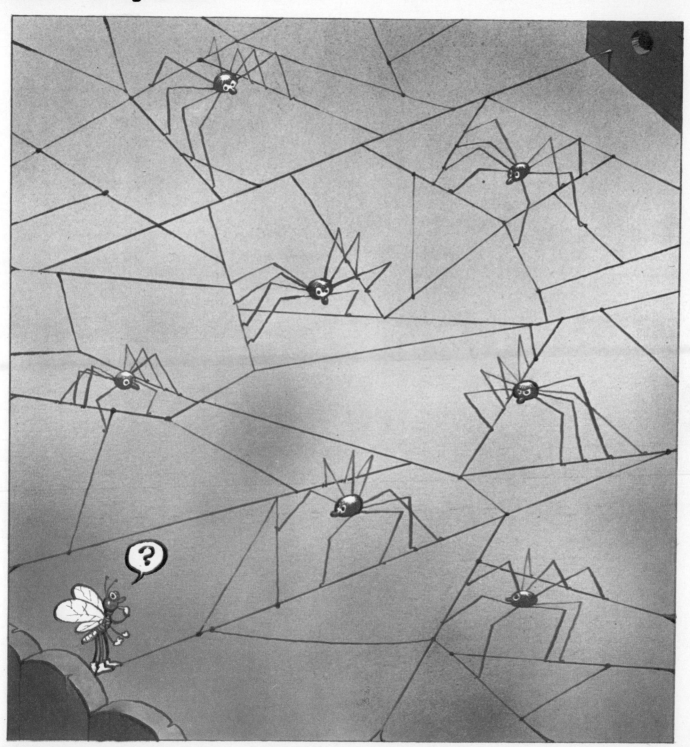

The fly is trying to find its way to safety in its hole in the wood. See if you can discover how it can avoid being trapped by the spiders. It must not touch any strands of the web where a spider is sitting. (The route is shown on the Answers pages at the back of the book.)

Giant match

Make a giant match appear out of a matchbox! Paint a **flat stick** about the size of a pencil with **paints** and a **paintbrush** to look like a matchstick. With scissors, cut one end from the drawer of a **matchbox**. Push the "match" up your sleeve so the head rests hidden in your palm.

★★★★ **Performance** ★★★★

Hold the matchbox half open with the open end toward you. With your other hand, pull the giant match from your sleeve up through the open end of the box facing your audience.

Bed of nails

In India, people called fakirs are able to sit on beds of nails. Tell your friends that you can sit on a bed of nails, too. No one will believe that you can do this dangerous trick!

★★★★ **Performance** ★★★★

With a **pencil** write the words "Bed of Nails" on a piece of **paper.** Now sit down on the paper. You've done just what you said you would do!

Wonder glass

Have you ever tried to balance something on your head? This balancing trick is easier but will leave your friends wondering how you did it.
1. Fold a piece of **cardboard** that is the same length as an **old playing card** into four sections, as shown. The two middle sections should be the same size, and wider than the two outside sections.

1

2. With **glue,** fix the two outside flaps to the back of the playing card so that the middle sections point outward. Make sure that the card stands up securely. **Ask an adult** if you may borrow a **small stemmed glass.**

2
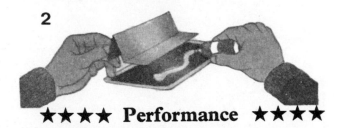

★★★★ **Performance** ★★★★

3. Fill the glass with **water** three-quarters full. Show your audience an **ordinary playing card,** identical to the original one. Then secretly switch it for the special card. Make sure your audience can't see behind the playing card. Balance the glass carefully so it rests on both the playing card and the card at the back.

3

Superstraw

Challenge a friend to lift a **narrow-necked bottle** by using only one drinking straw. When your friend gives up trying, you can do it easily. Be sure to practice a few times first.

1. Bend back about 1½ to 2 inches of one end of a **new drinking straw.** The straw will open again a bit.

1

2. Lower the bent end of the straw into the bottle until it passes the narrowest part of the neck and opens a little.

2

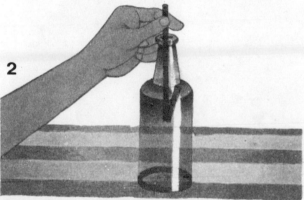

3. Pull the straw up until the tip of the bent end is wedged under the narrow neck. Now lift the straw and the bottle will lift up, too!

3

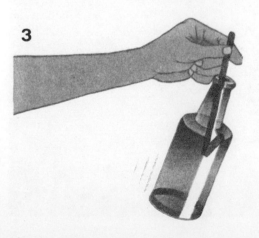

Inverted water

No one will believe that you can turn a glass full of water upside down – without spilling the water! Fill a **glass** with **water.** Lay a piece of **paper** across the top of the glass. Press the palm of your hand down on the paper. While pressing down with one hand, turn the glass upside down with the other hand. Press the paper for a couple of minutes more, and then take that hand away. Better practice this trick over the sink a few times! The paper will appear to hold the water in the glass. This is because the air under the glass is pressing against the paper with more pressure than the water is pressing against the paper.

Turning red

You can make a **violet** change its color. Violets have a chemical coloring that turns red in acid solutions. All you have to do is pour some **vinegar,** which contains acetic acid, onto a violet, and watch it turn red!

Walking clown

Here's a quick and easy way to make a clown that walks.
Draw the shape of a clown on **thin cardboard** with a **pencil.** Cut out the shape with **scissors.**
Paint clothes on your clown with **poster paints.**
Paint a funny face on your clown, or find a face you like in an old magazine. Cut it out and fix it on with **glue.**

Bend the feet forward so that they stand flat.
Cut two strips of **paper,** each about ¾ inch wide and about 2¾ inches long.
Roll them into tubes that fit your fingers. Glue the ends down.
Glue the tubes to the back of the legs.
Put your fingers into the tubes and make your clown walk!

2¾ ins

¾ inch

roll paper
into tube
and glue

glue
head to
body

glue tubes
to legs

Aloha

You can welcome your friends in the same way as the people in Hawaii do. They say "Aloha" (ah-lo-ha) and put garlands of flowers called *leis* (lay-ees) around people's necks.

1

2

FOLD
X
FOLD

FOLD
X
FOLD

3

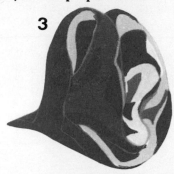

1. With **scissors,** cut **tissue paper** and **crepe paper** into squares of different sizes. Fold each square in half, and then in half again.

2. Trim around the cut edges of the squares to make some petals curved and some petals pointed.

3. Hold the point marked X and twist it around. Open out the flowers with your fingers. Curl and wrinkle the tissue a little.

4

5

4. Cut out lots of different leaf shapes from **green paper.**

5. Use a **darning needle** to thread the flowers and leaves onto a long piece of **yarn.**
Remove the needle and knot the ends of the yarn together.
Give a paper lei to a friend.

Aloha

Rocket balloon

If you blow up a balloon and let it go, it will fly crazily about the room. This project shows how to make a balloon fly in a straight line.

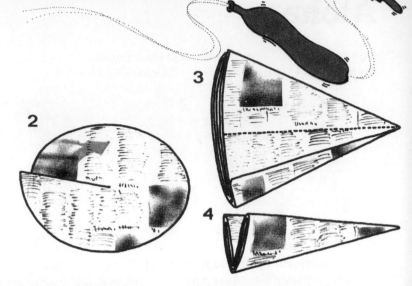

Fix a **thumbtack** into the fold of a sheet of **lightweight paper** about 32 inches x 26 inches.
1. Draw the biggest circle you can by using a pencil tied to string. (See Project 247.)

Cut out the circle with **scissors**. Cut along the fold from the edge to the center of the circle.
2. Overlap the paper and fold it around to make a cone shape about 8 inches in diameter at its base.

3. Flatten the cone with your hand to make a triangle. Fold the triangle in half.
4. Then fold the triangle in half again.

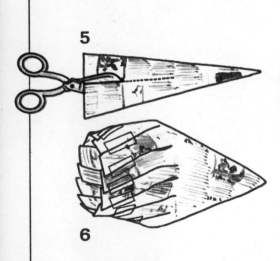

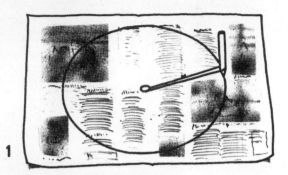

5. Cut from the base of the triangle halfway to the top. Open the shape to a cone again.
6. Overlap the cut sections and join them with **cellophane tape**.

Tie about 2 yards of **thread** to a **door handle**.
Slip a **straw** on the thread.
Tie the other end of the thread to a **chair**.
Tape the rocket to the straw.
Blow up a **sausage-shaped balloon.** Push it right inside the rocket. Now let go!

The air coming out of the balloon creates the energy needed to make the rocket move. The straw on the thread keeps the rocket flying in a straight line.
If you make several rockets you can have races with friends.

Uphill roller

This experiment shows how to make a roller move uphill, and explains how gravity makes it happen.

1. Curl a strip of **cardboard** about 22 inches by 4 inches into a ring.

2. With **cellophane tape,** join the ends together where they meet. (The ends should butt, or meet, not overlap.)
Put tape on both sides of the seam.

3. Tape a **small stone** inside the ring. (Use a stone no bigger than the width of the ring.)

4. Lay the ring on a sheet of **paper** and draw around it with a **pencil.**
(If you use tissue paper, you will be able to see the stone inside the roller.)

Cut out the paper circle with **scissors.**
Cut another paper circle in the same way.

5. With tape, fix a paper circle to each side of the cardboard ring.
Lean a piece of **stiff cardboard** on a **book** to make a slope.
Put the roller at the bottom of the slope.
If you position the roller so that the stone inside is as high as possible, the stone's weight will make the roller move uphill.

Gravity is the force that keeps all bodies moving downward, toward the center of the Earth. The stone is the roller's center of gravity, since it is much heavier than the rest of the roller. The roller moves uphill so as to make its center of gravity as low as possible.

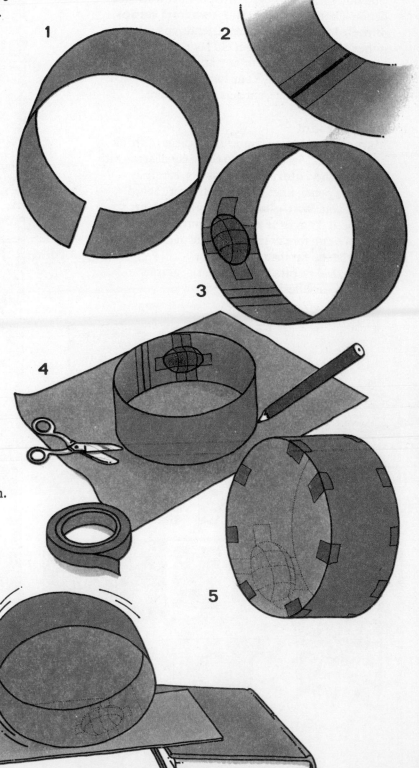

Space base

You don't have to be a scientist to have a science-fiction laboratory. Make your own from **scraps of metal.** Ask your parents, friends and relatives if they have any parts from old lawn mowers, bicycles, radios, clocks or any other machines that are no longer needed. Your local garage may give you some nuts, bolts, springs and washers.

Control room
Make a control room from a large piece of **thick cardboard.** Mark it off into three equal areas with a **pencil** and **ruler.** With **scissors,** carefully score the pencil lines and bend the cardboard toward you. With **glue,** fix **matchboxes or cardboard cartons** along the bottom of your control room for computers. Glue metal scraps along the top for instrument panels.
Use poster paints to make charts, graphs and space-age designs.

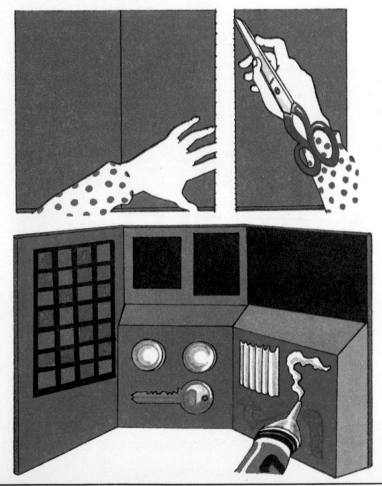

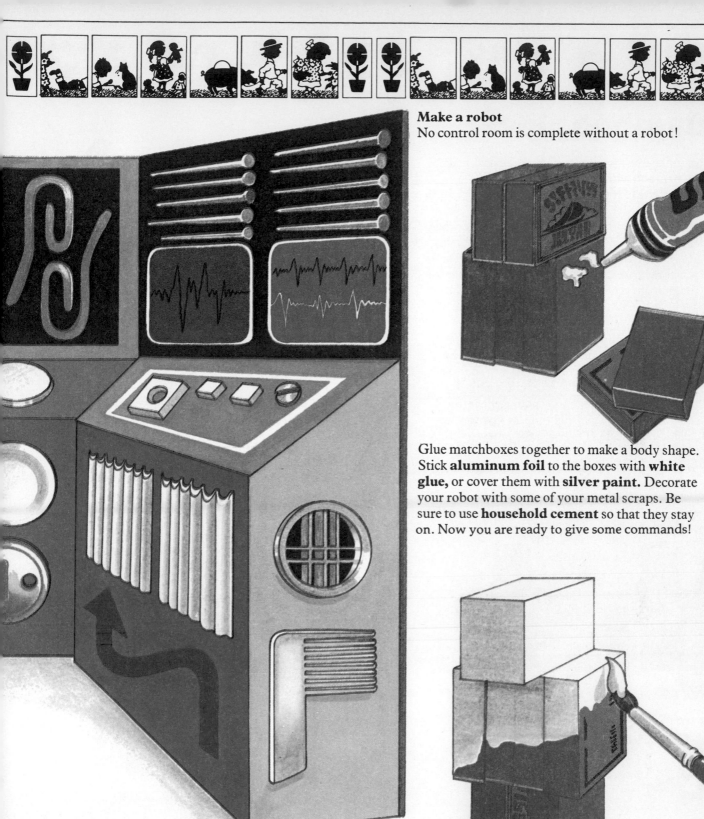

Make a robot
No control room is complete without a robot!

Glue matchboxes together to make a body shape. Stick **aluminum foil** to the boxes with **white glue,** or cover them with **silver paint.** Decorate your robot with some of your metal scraps. Be sure to use **household cement** so that they stay on. Now you are ready to give some commands!

Bamboo pipes

Pipes like these were played in Ancient Greece.
Buy bamboo with a large hole in the middle.

1. Ask an adult to cut 8½ inches off a long length
of **bamboo** with a **small saw.** Then cut seven
more lengths, each one about ½ inch shorter than
the previous one. Each piece should be cut at a
joint in the bamboo so it is closed at one end and
open at the other. You will also need one piece long
enough to go across the other eight pieces. Clean
out any pith from the middle of the bamboo.
Use **sandpaper** to even the open ends.
Blow across the open top of the longest of the
eight pieces while holding it vertically. Do the
same with the next piece. If it does not sound a
note higher than the first piece, cut it a bit
shorter, but not more than ¼ inch. Repeat this
until you have done all eight pieces giving you
an eight-note scale. These are the pipes.

2. Cut the long crosspiece in half lengthwise.
Put the eight pipes between the two lengths, with
all the openings at the same level.
Follow steps 3-8 carefully to tie your pipes and
crosspiece tightly together with **strong cord.**

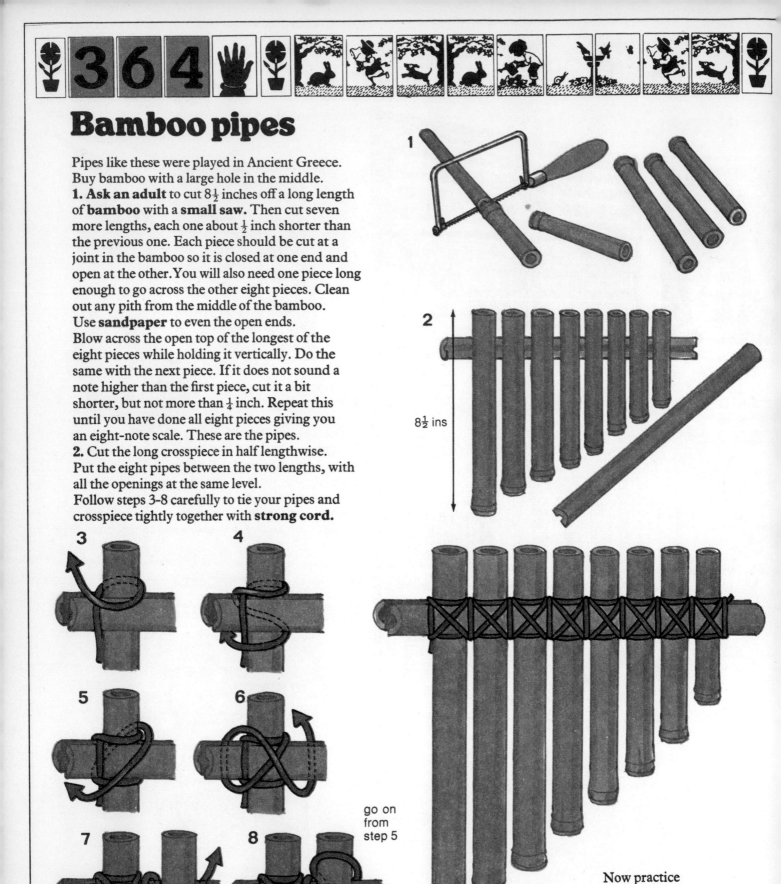

1

2

8½ ins

3

4

5

6

go on
from
step 5

7

8

Now practice
playing a tune!

Grass rabbits

You can make a rabbit for your brother or sister or a friend from tall, **flowering summer grasses.** This rabbit won't hop away!

1. Choose two medium-length grasses with flowers for ears. Bend a blade of grass around the stems below the ears to form the head. Wind **thread** around all the stems to hold them together.

1

2

3

4

2. Add one more grass at each side of the body so their flowers form the arms. Bind the stems with thread.

3. Using thread, bind a few long flowers around all the stems for the body.

4. Add small flowers for feet. Bind the grass stems securely. Add a tail the same way.

5. Bind all the stalks with thread so you can use them to hold up your rabbit.

6. Give your rabbit eyes with **thick paint.**

5

6

Answer pages

20.

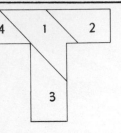

21. He takes the hen across to the bank. He returns alone. He then rows the fox across, leaves it, and brings back the hen. Then he takes the grain across, leaves it with the fox, and returns finally for the hen.

22.

42. Erect the post so the sign with the name of the village you have come from points down that road. Then the signs will be right.

43.

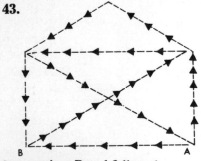

Start at A or B and follow the broken lines.

44. The pairs are: $1+9, 2+8, 4+12, 5+14, 7+13, 10+16$. There are four odd cars left.

45. Rhinoceros, donkey, tiger, shark, turtle, kangaroo.

46. The triangles are: ABC, ABD, ABE, ABF, ABG, ABH, ACD, ACE, ACI, ADE, ADH, AEF, AEG, AEI, AFG, BCD, BCE, BCG, BCH, BCJ, BDE, BDF, BEJ, BGH, CDE, CDH, CDI, CDJ, CEG, CHJ, DEF, DEI, DEJ, DIJ, EFI.

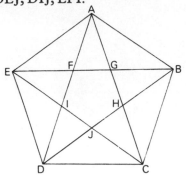

70.

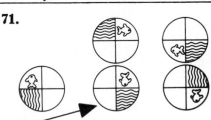

71.

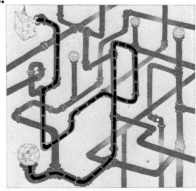

This fish is the odd one out because it is swimming in a counter clockwise direction from the sea, instead of clockwise.

72.

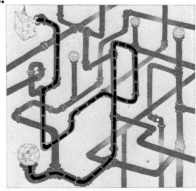

103. a,g,f,c,h,b,e,d.

104. Eleven.

105. He lets air out of each tire until the truck sinks by 1 inch.

106.

122. The star, because all the others are household objects.

123. Eight, because the numbers increase by $+1$, $+2$, $+3$, $+4$, $+5$.

124. Knot all three together so that they form a circle.

125.

Push your friend's string *under* the loop on your wrist. Make the loop big enough so that you can slip it over your hand.

126. Empty the second bucket into the fifth, and then return it to its original position.

127.

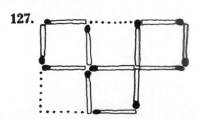

144.

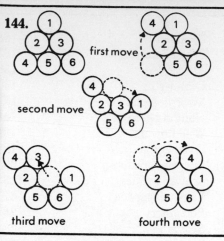

first move

second move

third move   fourth move

145. Coconut, bananas, pear, apple, lemon, fig, cherries.

146. The big Eskimo is the little Eskimo's mother.

147. Sailor (e), American Indian (c), cowpuncher (f), Oriental (b), clown (a), football player (d).

148.

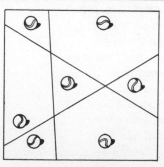

149.

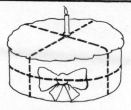

176. Addis Ababa, New York, Madrid, Sydney, Delhi, Paris.

177. 1 +22, 2 +5, 3 +20, 4 +18, 6 +14, 7 +19, 8 +12, 9 +17, 10 +13, 11 +21, 15 +16.

204. Tree, butterfly, airplane.

205.

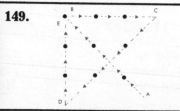

206. The first boy changes place with the other boy, and stands on his head to form 49!

207. A wristwatch.

234.

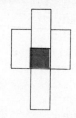

256. It hasn't actually disappeared. There are only nine lines on each triangle. By sliding them together you make the lines longer.

257.

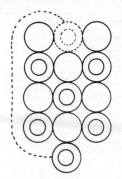

Move the middle coin as shown, then push up the whole row of coins.

283.

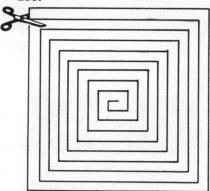

Starting at the top left-hand corner, cut around and around as shown. Hold the ends of the paper and stretch it out.

304. Number three. Try it and see!

305. The number seven is the odd one out as it is the only numeral.

306. l,f,e,b,a,d,g,c.

307. 1. Greece, 2.Spain, 3.Holland, 4.Wales, 5.Japan, 6.Mexico.

330. The squares are: ABJH, ACQO, BCGJ, BGPH, DEJI, DFNL, EFKJ, HJPO, IJML, JGQP, JKNM.

The triangles are: ABH, ACO, BFC, BCG, BCJ, BEF, BFJ, BJG, BDF, DBE, DFL, EFJ, FCG, HBJ, HOL, HDI, HIL, HJL, HJO, HJP, HLD, HPO, IJL, JCG, JFK, KFG, LFN, LJM, LMP, MNP, NFG, NKG, OCQ, OJP, OLP, PGQ, PJG, PLN.

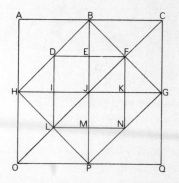

331. The third hunter was right. They each ate $2\frac{2}{3}$ sandwiches ($8 \div 3$). The first hunter gave the third hunter $2\frac{1}{3}$ sandwiches ($=\frac{2}{3}$) and the second one gave him one third of a sandwich ($=\frac{1}{3}$). So the ratio is seven cents to one cent.

351. Aladdin, Snow White and the Seven Dwarfs, Puss-in-Boots.

352.

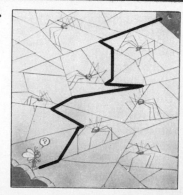

Project guide

All 365 projects are grouped under the *kind* of project, identified by its color code, with the number of the project next to each one. Find your favorite kind of project, then look under the headings to see which ones are easy, not-so-easy or harder, and if there are any that need an adult's help.

Magic

Easy

Not-so-easy

Harder

Nature

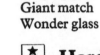

Easy

Not-so-easy

Harder

Ask an adult

Science

★ Easy

★★ Not-so-easy

★★★ Harder

✋ Ask an adult

Crafts

★ Easy

★★ Not-so-easy

★★★ Harder

✋ Ask an adult

Hobbies

★ Easy

★★ Not-so-easy